Praise for the documentary feature film
Voices in Wartime

"*Voices in Wartime* is a thoughtful, provocative exploration of the ways poets have dealt with the experience of battle throughout history. The words of Homer, Emily Dickinson, Wilfred Owen and Langston Hughes as well as a scribe from ancient Babylonia and contemporary writers are read with eloquence against a backdrop of disturbing images from actual combat footage and from fiction films, to produce a searing chronicle of the effects of armed conflict on humanity." — *Los Angeles Times*

"Along with wor   affecting images
of soldiers and c   o quickly, really.
This is a film tha   ssing from the
national convers

"Side by side, in   03 invasion of
Iraq and the wo   nt not only about
the devastation   *New York Times*

"No choral lame   locumentary is
rather a frank di   from historical
conflicts becaus   geographically
defined battlegr   teral damage,"
the women and   ook on — can
highlight the fol   ed 'the
blood-swollen C

"An overview of   in Wartime
touches upon H   alt Whitman's
lyrical account c   ldier-poets as
Siegfried Sassoo   erse of Vietnam
vet David Conn

"A history of ver   they are braided
together proves   war, but it isn't
always provided   suggests
soldiers in battl   other during
combat duress.   her battle against
fear that rages w   es as more than
a string of fine,

"… a moving documentary about poetry inspired by combat." — *New York Post*

"Poetry… is the literary form best suited to capturing the intense, often contradictory emotions of battlefield experiences that noncombatants can never entirely comprehend. That vividness is a compelling reason for this short documentary — filled with some of the most powerful poetry and shattering images ever to come out of warfare — to be required viewing for any one who believes him- or herself outside war's reach." — *TV Guide's Movie Guide*

"…one of the most original war movies ever made…Men die miserably every day for lack of what is found there." — Seattle Weekly

"It's interesting that, in a documentary about war poetry that supplements literary readings with the occasional use of exceedingly bloody archival war footage, the words more than hold their own against the pictures." — *The Washington Post*

"With such euphemisms as "ultimate sacrifice" and "collateral damage" flying fast and furious, language often takes a direct hit in time of war. This bracing documentary celebrates the ways poets through the ages offer antidotes to the double-speak, restoring meaning to language with their protests and observations." — *The Hollywood Reporter*

"*Voices in Wartime* is smart, angry, and unflinching, an admirable cinematic elaboration on [Wilfred] Owen's maxim that 'true poets must be truthful.'" — *Washington City Paper*

"*Voices in Wartime* may prove to be the most startlingly literate document of war ever created for film. Director Rick King … interweaves passages of war-themed poetry — new and old; from the famous, the infamous, and the unheard of — with stock footage and stills from these violent episodes of our past. The montage features disembodied voiceovers reciting both graphic and beautiful literary works from the likes of Langston Hughes, Emily Dickinson, Walt Whitman, and Siegfried Sassoon; coupled with interviews from a host of historians, soldiers, and experts which all work to illustrate how war and poetry are invariably intertwined. The editing is crisp, often layering upon itself an array of images with interviews and narrative." — *San Francisco Bay Guardian*

VOICES IN WARTIME

Voices in Wartime Anthology
Edited by Andrew Himes with
Jan Bultmann and others
Cover illustration by Kim Francisco
Design by Tracy Lamb
Copyright 2005 © Andrew Himes

Published by Whit Press, Inc. Whit Press
Richard Hugo House 1634 Eleventh Avenue
Seattle, WA 98122 www.whitpress.org

ISBN 0-9720205-3-5
Library of Congress Control Number:
2005923275

VOICES IN WARTIME

ANTHOLOGY

A Collection of Narratives and Poems

Edited by Andrew Himes
with Jan Bultmann and others

ACKNOWLEDGMENTS

Rick King was the miraculous director of *Voices in Wartime*, an extraordinary film created by a filmmaker with passion, integrity, and enormous skill. Without Rick's vision, talent, commitment and willingness to take one of the biggest risks of his career, you would not now be reading this book. Rick conducted over forty hours of interviews upon which most of the narratives are based, and devoted his life at much personal sacrifice for almost a year to creating the film.

Jonathan King, who produced the film *Voices in Wartime* together with his brother Rick, poured his whole heart into the film, spent hundred of hours in research and project management, set up the logistics and guided the development and production process. Without Jonathan's passion for excellence, his ability to juggle tasks, and his understanding of the role of the artist in helping us understand the experience of war, neither the film nor this book would have seen the light of day.

Jan Bultmann was the heart of the team that produced this book. She managed a large team of volunteers who edited the film transcripts for publication on the web site *voicesinwartime.org* and in this book. She directly edited a large section of the book herself, and she kept us on schedule and happy with each other.

For hours spent transcribing interviews with patience and care, special thanks to Jonathan King, Kathryn Linehan, and Alix Wilber. For editing the transcriptions with attention and speed, thanks to Jan Bultmann, Michelle Byrd, James Crowley, Rebecca Gleason, Jeff Hannibal, Nancy Matthew, Ken Milne, Handan Selamoglu, Mary Sobczyk, Holly Thomas, Laura Williams, and Chris Cavanaugh.

For sifting through reams of personal narratives and poems and creating order, thanks to Handan Selamoglu. For finalizing sections, Sheila Sebron, Diane Stielstra, Jan Bultmann, Chris Cavanaugh. For a life-saving copy edit, Elise Daniel. For proofing the final copy, Kathleen Atkins.

For the beauty of the design of this book, thanks to Tracy Lamb of Whit Press, and for unfailing encouragement and enthusiasm, as well as squeezing hours and minutes and days out of the schedule, thanks to Claudia Mauro, also of Whit Press.

For their stories, their ideas, their art, and their generous gift of time, thanks to all those who agreed to be interviewed for the film *Voices in Wartime*, and whose narratives and poetry appear in this book.

Finally, Alix Wilber lived this project and shaped every part of it. Thanks to her for filling my life with light and poodles and ideas.

— Andrew Himes

TABLE OF CONTENTS

INTRODUCTION

—Andrew Himes

From my childhood I lived in the middle of the idea of war, trapped between the World War II memories of my parents and my own terror of the imminence of World War III. I was born just before the outbreak of the Korean War and came to young adulthood as the Vietnam War spiraled toward its senseless and incomprehensibly bloody conclusion.

As a boy in Tennessee, I fought imaginary battles against my brother Johnny's own imaginary army, from foxhole to foxhole through a field of Johnson grass, with plastic rifles and cherry bombs as weapons. My favorite weekly television program in the early '60s was *Combat*, in which Vic Morrow led a squad of exhausted, heroic, unshaven, hardened yet tender, fierce and frightened, and above all very human American soldiers through the French countryside in search of the German army in the aftermath of the Normandy landing. A decade later, my favorite program was *M.A.S.H.*, in which a bitterly funny Army surgeon patches up the wounded while railing against the ironies and stupidities of the Korean War.

Between *Combat* and *M.A.S.H.*, I grew up on the nightly bad news from Vietnam—Walter Cronkite reporting via *CBS News* on another village destroyed with its inhabitants in a B-52 strike, or another platoon of U.S. soldiers decimated by an enemy ambush, or another 39 or 412 or 16 bodies of "communist sympathizers" tallied as part of an ever expanding kill count, or another grenade tossed into a Saigon nightclub by a Viet Cong guerrilla.

I'm not a pacifist. That is, I've always been able to imagine how the use of military force might be required to prevent or mitigate crimes against humanity—to interdict Hitler's holocaust of the Jews, or stop the mass murder in Rwanda, or prevent the destruction of a skyscraper by a madman in an airliner. But I've also believed that most wars are preventable—caused by human error or avariciousness, ambition or cupidity, or by human pathology, or by plain evil. And I've believed it's possible to minimize wars by addressing the root causes of war—by alleviating poverty, suffering and resentment, and by building more equitable and sustainable societies.

We can only decide wisely whether or not to go to war only if we truly understand the human cost and experience of war, the emotional reality of war. My decision, as the invasion of Iraq rolled toward Baghdad in 2003, was to make a film, *Voices in Wartime*, which would use the words and stories of poets and other writers who have been through war's crucible to explore that reality. I hoped that if all of us truly understood the trauma of war we might choose differently the next time we confront our options. But the film is a meditation on war, a reflection on war's cost and lasting trauma—not a statement of opposition to any particular policy or political decision of my government. It is an attempt to get at the heart of war itself.

We've inherited a world whose history reeks of blood and mayhem, suffused by the odors and emotions of war. We live in a world riven by violent conflict and its echoes, rumblings, sorrows, threats, and unforeseen consequences. We face a future, inevitably, in which war will be an engine of human politics, history, and possibility.

The central lesson I learned through the production of the film *Voices in Wartime* was that one fundamental reason for the persistence of war as a human activity is the trauma suffered by both individuals and societies through acts of collective violence. So a simple answer is that war itself helps to create the conditions that nurture successive wars. In the end, we will move beyond war only when we learn how to heal that trauma, and then how to imagine alternatives to war.

In this book, through the eyes of poets, war correspondents, doctors, soldiers, and historians, we examine the phenomenon of war. Fear and sorrow, the terrible suffering and distortions of character that emerge from the experience of war, the lasting trauma and the need for healing—all these are explored in the narratives that follow, based on interviews conducted for the film *Voices in Wartime*.

It becomes clear from reading these narratives and poems that the most powerful expositor of war is someone who has seen war firsthand and whose authentic voice can best tell the story. For a warrior, the act of writing about the trauma of war is an attempt to transmute the pain into something else: not relief, necessarily, or transcendence, and certainly not glory, but maybe a kind of understanding, especially if there is someone else who can hear the story with compassion and acceptance. This may be so because witnessing war's suffering creates the need to speak about what one has seen, while it may also prevent the witness from speaking.

Many combat veterans have taken part in or observed deeds that have silenced them—deeds too shameful or impossible or morally ambiguous to explain to others, civilians, who have not shared the experience of the warrior. As Jonathan Shay (a psychiatrist and writer featured in the film *Voices in Wartime*) explains, for a combat veteran who feels compelled to remain mute, the price might be a continuing rage—for years or a lifetime—a sundering or crippling of relationships, a diminished capacity to love and accept love. So war exacts a toll from its participants that is deeper and more lasting than any physical injury.

Poetry itself may be the tool of alchemy best able to contain the contradiction of the experience of war—the terrible beauty, the pity, the heightened struggle between life and death. Vietnamese soldier-poet Nguyen Duy expressed this contradiction well in this line: "The maddening agony, the honey comes from within."

Somewhere in the dark, nestled between the story and the silence, is the beginning of our healing.

— Andrew Himes

Part 1:

PERSPECTIVES

José Diaz is a poet, soldier, and father of two. He returned to the U.S. in the fall of 2004 after serving a year's deployment in Iraq as a military police sergeant in the Army Reserves. He wrote this poem as a reflection on his life in a combat zone, and how that experience—including frequent mortar attacks, improvised explosive devices, car bombs, and his interactions with both Iraqis and fellow soldiers—changed him "for good."

A Prayer for Relief

José Diaz

~

I feel more lucid now and then, but at times, I feel the creeping signs
Of a premature senility, the runaway tremor, the starlit humming
    of the ears.
I drive aimlessly in circles, lacking focus, fumbling for change as my
    breath freezes,
Like the dust storm that overwhelms the ceaseless chatter of the
    airport lounge.

It's like I never left the cold comfort of my cot, as if I were the
    signatory still
To some unwritten, ill-advised rules of engagement, some ancient
    code of my design.
I see myself at the ready, quick to pounce on the dignity of a man
    begging me
With his weary walk for the honor of shining my own long lost,
    tasseled walk.

Yet I feel pouring through my rehearsed gaze the distant cousin
    of my self-control,

The mastery of a sense unknown, the art of comprehension
  of the fearless word.
It is a sword unrepentant that I sheath in the soft folds of my
  corrected smile,
Another truce it bleeds upon the false report of our most
  irreverent embrace.

Unbidden come to stay my gait the lurid whispers of a languid
  autumn night,
Echoes that flit unbound in the arctic hue, the unforgiving joy
  of city lights.

Chris Hedges is a former New York Times war correspondent with 15 years of experience in places such as El Salvador, Kosovo, and the Persian Gulf. He shared in a 2002 Pulitzer Prize for coverage of global terrorism. This narrative was adapted from Chris Hedges' interview with Rick King for the documentary film Voices in Wartime.

The Collective Madness

Chris Hedges

The reality of combat is nothing like the image I think many of us carry into combat. First of all, there's the factor of fear, which is overpowering in situations where violent death is all around you. Fear is something which you have a constant second-by-second, minute-by-minute, hour-by-hour battle to control. You always have moments in which fear takes control and in which you fail, in which your instincts towards self-preservation make you crumble. And anybody (including soldiers coming out of combat) who tells you otherwise is not telling you the truth.

It's a constant battle against fear. There are always times when fear wins. Courage is not a state. Courage is an act. And I think one of the reasons that those who carry out what we would define as courageous acts are often very reticent to speak about it afterward is because they're not completely sure they could do it again.

A War Correspondent's View

Most of my adult life has been spent as a war correspondent. I started in El Salvador where I spent five years covering the civil war there as well as in Nicaragua and Guatemala. After a sabbatical to study Arabic, I went to Jerusalem, covered the first Intifada (or Palestinian uprising) as well as the cancellation of the elections in Algeria and the rise of the Algerian insurgency, and the civil war in the Sudan.

I went on to cover the Persian Gulf War. It was after the war at the Shiite uprising in Basra, and I was taken prisoner for eight days by the Iraqi Republican Guard. I became the Middle East bureau chief out of Cairo for the *New York Times* and spent a lot of time with the Kurds in northern Iraq, and a lot of time with the Shiites in southern Iraq during the insurgency. I covered the civil war in Yemen and then in Sarajevo in 1995 and covered the end of the war in Bosnia and the war in Kosovo. So, most of my life has been spent abroad as a war correspondent.

Once you are in combat and often a few seconds after you enter it, it is nothing like you expect it will be. But more importantly, you realize that you are not the person you thought you were. It is a constant second-by-second, minute-by-minute battle against your own fear and that overpowering urge for self-protection, which in combat sometimes only puts you in a more precarious situation. For instance when you are mortared, mortars spray out in a kind of conical shape, and your natural tendency is to get up and run which is very dangerous. You have to lie down because even with a mortar impact coming relatively close to you, if you are very close to the ground or hopefully in a ditch or behind a tree, that spray, that circular spray of shrapnel may not hit you. If you got up and ran, it would. I saw a lieutenant get killed in El Salvador. He got a piece of shrapnel the size of a dime up through the bottom of his chin. When we looked at his body, we couldn't even see a mark on it.

There are times in combat when you lose, and anyone who tells you otherwise is lying. There are always moments when fear overtakes you and you can't function. Images that are peddled so often in media, in movies, and in novels of heroics, such as running out to save a wounded comrade, feel very different when you're in combat. It's very confusing. You don't know what's happening around you and it's a constant struggle to figure out where the shots are coming from, where a zone of safety is that you can get to, how you should react. You are aware of a very, very tiny area in your immediate vicinity, and you're not really aware of what's happening anywhere else.

I think that Tolstoy in *War and Peace* managed to write quite effectively about this notion that you may be engaged in a grand battle that has perhaps even historic significance, but you yourself know almost nothing even though you're in the midst of it. In combat, you don't know what you're witnessing. Modern combat is organized industrial slaughter with extremely powerful weapons that have the ability to descend on you from a great distance. In modern combat, we often never see our attackers, even when we are using relatively unsophisticated weapons such as automatic assault rifles.

Although I spent five years covering the war in El Salvador, it was very rare that I ever saw who was shooting at me. Once you get into a situation like the Iraq War or the Persian Gulf War or in Bosnia where you're using very large weapons—tanks, 155 howitzers— these weapons have the capacity to fire from several miles away, and that is the predominating fact of modern warfare. It is largely and almost completely impersonal. Those who fire at you cannot see you and you cannot see your attackers, and the caliber and size of the weapons means that large numbers of people have the capacity to die in an instant without ever seeing where that firing is coming from. That is the reality of the modern battlefield. This has become even more true since modern industrial warfare was invented in the First World War.

There has become more of a need for the myth of individual heroics—what the Army calls the "Army of One" in its commercials— as though "the lie" of an individual or the role of an individual on a battlefield has become more pronounced. By "the lie," I mean that an individual can somehow really change the course of a battle. When you've been through an experience of combat in modern industrial warfare, you realize how patently ridiculous and absurd that is. Technology rules battlefields.

I suffered from, and probably still suffer from, post-traumatic stress disorder. I think people who spend as much time as I have around organized violence bear the scars of that violence and probably will bear them for the rest of their lives. It's not something you escape.

How does it affect you? At its height it makes you very paranoid, very jumpy. I remember leaving Sarajevo at the height of the siege to go to Paris where I would be able to get a good night's sleep and try to recharge my batteries for returning. And as I would walk down the street in Paris, it's as if I saw everything around me from the end of a long tunnel. I couldn't relate. I couldn't wait to get back to the world at war because I couldn't function any longer in a world not at war.

I needed to be with those comrades who understood the trauma and emotional mutilation that I was undergoing. Somehow I needed that drug in order to function. It's, of course, a very self-destructive drug. But a very real one. And I think it's why you see war correspondents or soldiers clamor to get back into situations that—if they were healthy—they would not want to go back to.

My Comrade, Myself

The first time that I was in an ambush where people were being shot was in the Salvadoran town of Suchitoto. This was a government outpost in a small town of mud and wattle huts off the main road. We drove up to a bridge and on the other side was a long stretch of asphalt surrounded by high grass, which was one of the most dangerous spots in the country at the time. The photographers stopped at the bridge to get high, which they found to be a necessary balm to their nerves. We went down the road with the odd shot being fired in front of or behind us until we got into the town.

Then we hooked up with a group of Salvadoran rebels who were accustomed to the follies of the press and moved up to this garrison that was completely surrounded in the center of Suchitoto. As we rounded a corner, several bursts of automatic weapons fire rent the air, and the rebels I was with began to fire back. Bullets hit the wall. There was a rebel who was very badly wounded and who started crying out for his mother, which was not uncommon with kids who were badly wounded. I remember his cries at first sort of haunted me and then I wished he would be quiet.

As I dove into the dirt to take cover, it obliterated in an instant that mythic perception of war that I had. I realized that war would always control me, that I would never control it. I felt humiliated, because I felt powerless and weak. I realized I was not the person I thought I was in the sense that I thought that I would react with courage and resolve instead of shaking in utter terror, praying. I prayed, saying, "God, if you get me out of here I will never do this again." And what happened when I got out? Like most war correspondents, I considered it a great cosmic joke and drank away my fear and excitement in a bar in downtown San Salvador that night.

This is part of the allure of war: Those of us who can control our fear go back and seek out that kind of a situation again and again and again. Winston Churchill said in his book *The River War*, there is nothing quite as exhilarating as being shot at without success. And it's a high, it's a rush, and you flirt with it. It's a dangerous, frightening game, but one you can become addicted to.

The longer you spend in war, the more deformed you become, and the harder it is to return to a society not at war, until finally death itself comes as a kind of release. There's no shortage of war correspondents, and I think of my friend Kurt Schork who was killed in Sierra Leone with another friend of mine, Miguel Gilmoreno—and another friend, Elizabeth Neuffer from *The Boston Globe*, who died in Iraq after the war. They knew they had to stop, but they kept going back to seek one more hit until it finally killed them.

And I did the same. After leaving Kosovo, I found myself back in Gaza and got caught in a very bad ambush in Gaza where there was a young Palestinian kid killed about 15 feet away from me. I realized I had to break free, I had to let go. None of this would or could or should come back. I was lucky to get out alive.

My friend Kurt did not. Kurt was killed in Sierra Leone in May of 2000 in an ambush, and that was a devastating blow for me. I had worked with Kurt for 10 years, starting in Iraq. He was literate and funny. The brave are often funny. He and I passed books back and forth to try to make sense of the mayhem all around us, and his loss is a hole that will never be filled. In some way because Kurt was who he was, there are parts of my existence that I will never be able to articulate to anyone ever again. It wasn't just that Kurt was there; other people were there too. It's that Kurt was one of the rare people who actually thought about it and understood it and tried to dissect it.

For three or four days after his death, I couldn't even drive a car. I was completely wiped out. I went, finally, to Sarajevo where his ashes are buried along with victims of the war and went to his grave and recited a poem Catullus wrote to honor his own brother who died. The question of whether Kurt died in vain is one I never asked. The fact is he died. And he died because he could not resist the pull of the very dark forces, the forces of war that called for his own extinction.

I admire, respect, and maybe even love war correspondents. They are the people whom I lived with for almost 20 years of my life.

But I also know how messed up they are. And how messed up I was. And I respect what they do and the courage and it takes and their integrity. On the other hand, it's painful to see that self-destructive urge engulf them. For those of us who leaped from war to war to war, it was finally that self-destructive urge that was predominant and had taken over lives, and it almost killed me. I broke free from it, and I can only view the loss of friends like Kurt as tragic. I can't justify it as being worthwhile or not having been in vain. Deaths that are not in vain are precisely the kind of clichés and rhetoric that disgust me when we talk about war. War is tragic, only tragic. The death of comrades and friends in war is a tragedy.

The Worship of Death

War is necrophilia. That's all it is. It's about the worship of death. We ennoble self-sacrifice for the other, for our comrade. It's called death. It's an illusion that somehow those comrades are bound to us in any real way. Think what it means to die for a friend.

When you are at war, you have the illusion that your comrades are one entity. That illusion is made a mockery of once the war ends, of course, because these comrades immediately become, again, strangers to us. And there is a suppression of self-awareness, self-expression among comrades that is, in the end, the very opposite of friendship. And that's why friendship or love is the great enemy of war. The failure that we make is to confuse this comradeship with friendship.

Friends do not do love the way comrades do love, death, and sacrifice. Friendship is about heightened self-awareness. We see ourselves through the eyes of a friend. We understand that inner core of being through a friend. And the loss of a friend means that dialogue that we have made will never be re-created with another. When you see veterans gathered together, they're not trying to re-create the suffering and horror of war, which they hate, perhaps in a way that only those who have been to war can hate. They are trying to re-create comradeship—that sense of inclusiveness, that sense of belonging and unity, in lives that since the war have probably been very solitary—but they can't. And that is part of war's great draw, the comradeship of the crowd. Once we are embraced by the crowd, once we have sacrificed all for the god of war, we become in the service of death, not life. That, ultimately, is what war demands of us.

Everyone is susceptible to the comradeship of war. Nobody's immune. That sense of comradeship is pervasive throughout a society in wartime. In Sarajevo, I sat after the war with friends who did not wish back the suffering, and, of course, I knew them when they were living in unheated apartments and didn't have water to bathe in or drink. But they also looked at me with a kind of despair because these were, perhaps, the fullest moments of their lives. And they wished it back, and I did too.

What they wished back wasn't real. It was part of the illusion of war. And it was an illusion that had filled up the void of an empty and sterile and futile present. They were all aware of the mockery of war, the mockery of their idealism. And the nationalist leaders who had gotten them into the mess in the first place, had grown rich off of their suffering, and were still in power. They were no longer lionized by actors and politicians who would come and visit Sarajevo during the cease-fires. But it was a moment, on some level, they will spend the rest of their lives longing to re-create. Part of the enticement and power of war is that it can create these kinds of feelings within human communities that probably cannot be replicated any other way.

Portrayals of War in Film and Literature

We don't hear enough about war from the perspective of the victims. And the only way to understand war is to understand it through the eyes of the victims. That's where the portrayals of war have really failed us. We see it through the eyes of the combatants, primarily.

I can think of a few examples that show us war as it is from those who bear the brunt of it. The Italian novelist Elsa Morantes's *History: A Novel*. Or a really great French film by René Clément, *Jeux interdits* or *Forbidden Games*, which was filmed in the early '50s, after the end of World War II. It has only one image of combat: It's at the beginning where German planes strafe a column of French refugees and kill the parents of a little girl. The rest of the movie is about this little girl now living orphaned in a village, trying to cope with the idea that her parents are buried under the ground. And with another little boy, against the backdrop of war, she buries things. They create cemeteries.

This is an insight into the way war brutalizes individuals, societies, and children. The fact is that when you see images of violence, they have a pornographic quality that is enticing, even war movies that are meant to denounce war, such as *Platoon*, for instance. In Anthony Swofford's memoir of the first Persian Gulf War called *Jar Head*, he writes about how he and other soldiers would rent these movies with cases of beer and watch them over and over and over. For soldiers, all of it was war porn.

But I think that's true not just for soldiers. It's like trying to make movies against pornography and showing erotic love scenes. You can't do it. Even those attempts to make antiwar films, for instance, *All Quiet on the Western Front*, I think people see it and feel, "I would like to be tested like that," or "I should be tested like that," or "I would like that kind of comradery even though war is horrible." That's very difficult to fight.

The Iliad could have been written in Bosnia. In Bosnia, you had vain, selfish, insensitive warlords who were quite willing to sacrifice their own for personal gain and personal pride. And that is the story of *The Iliad*. *The Iliad* understands the pettiness, narrowness, and almost maniacal obsession of those who command, and how they are quite willing to see their own slaughtered for what, in the end, are absolutely absurd reasons.

Achilles is, in my reading of *The Iliad*, a distorted and deformed figure. He is attacked by Agamemnon, by Nestor, and by others because as they say, he actually *likes* war. There's a realization that as glorious a warrior as he is, these are qualities that have no place in a civil society. There is no society for Achilles to return to because the very qualities that find him exalted on the battlefield are completely out of place off the battlefield.

That's the story of *The Odyssey*. *The Odyssey* is Odysseus's 10-year attempt at recovery, to curb his warrior's heart. It's a long and difficult struggle. There's a wonderful scene in *The Odyssey* where Odysseus descends to the underworld and meets Achilles. Achilles said, "I'd rather be a serf pounding out clods of dirt on some farm above than here in the house of death." I think *The Iliad*, because of its understanding of the motives of war and brutality—and there are very graphic descriptions of the slaughter of death—coupled with *The Odyssey*, which is an attempt by Odysseus to reintegrate himself into civil society, are a searing indictment of war, the culture of war, and what it does to individuals and societies.

It's a searing indictment because the writer, Homer, or writers under the name of Homer, understood what war was. And they knew what they were writing about. They understood the warrior caste. They understood comradeship and the danger of comradeship. They understood the capriciousness of fate. They understood the indifference of the gods.

The characters in *The Iliad* and *The Odyssey* live in a morally neutral universe. The gods switch sides with amazing rapidity in the war, sometimes choosing favorites on the battlefield and then suddenly abandoning them. I think that gives us a much, much more realistic vision of the deadly neutrality of nature, especially in wartime.

War results in the destruction of the moral code. In war everything is turned upside down. Decency, sobriety, and honesty no longer pay. Those who give themselves up to the lust of war triumph in war. When we see flashes of human nobility or let's say human morality, whether it's with Hector and Andromache or with King Priam coming to beg for the body of Hector in Achilles's tent, we're reminded of the perverse world that war is. The essence of war is death. Everything in a wartime culture calls us to sacrifice on the altar for the god of war. We begin by sacrificing others. But when we stay long enough in war, we end up by sacrificing ourselves.

Any time human beings find themselves in moments or periods of extreme deprivation or suffering they turn away from the trivia that dominates our airwaves and our lives. Those who can articulate something beneath the surface glitter that most of us ingest day and night—great poets, musicians, artists, writers, all of those artists who struggle in a profound way with the human condition—suddenly have something to say to us as we struggle, Job-like, with whatever horrors we're undergoing.

Poetry has always been a part of war. In every war that I've covered, soldiers write poetry. I was with a battalion of Marines in the Persian Gulf War and a lance corporal had written a poem about making a phone call to his mother and hearing his mother cry on the other end of the phone. And it was maudlin and sentimental. I think it was Oscar Wilde who said, "All bad poetry is sincere." But it really struck home with these kids. And almost everyone in his battalion had memorized the poem. I think that's typical in wartime.

But we should be very clear that there are usually two types of artistic endeavor in wartime: At the inception of a war most artists, including poets, are more than happy to lend themselves to the war effort. Even great minds like Freud and Thomas Mann supported the folly of the First World War. Then there is within artists and within poets a kind of conversion during the war process, and they begin to portray combat as it really is.

Some of them never really convert. Kipling lent his jingoistic talents (it's a little unfair, I mean, I actually like Kipling) to the war effort and to the glory of the empire, until, of course, his son, for whom he secured a commission, was killed. Then Kipling couldn't write much at all after that. It shattered his conception of empire, military life, and glory.

Poets, writers, and artists are just as susceptible to the euphoric intoxication of war as the rest of us. And I think they are perhaps more willing and predisposed to lend their talents to the war effort because they live more on the margins of society. So you have great painters like Christopher Nevinson, who painted the shells they fire at night to light up a battlefield as abstract starbursts, beautiful geometric shapes. Finally, at the end of the war, Nevinson's great painting *Paths of Glory*, which is not abstract at all but very realistic, shows two British soldiers with their bodies tangled up in barbed wire outside a trench. It is a painting, of course, that was immediately censored by the British government. Nevinson hung it in a show with a brown wrapper over the painting and wrote "Censored" across it.

Artists and writers who are willing to lend their talents to the war effort are highly prized because they are some of the most creative minds in our society, and they know how to manipulate public perceptions. But when they turn on the war, they are often swiftly silenced.

Our images of war are completely choreographed, of course, and sanitized, immensely sanitized. They bear no relationship at all to the reality of war—to the point of lunacy. The notion that somehow watching *Saving Private Ryan* has anything to do with experiencing actual combat is silly. The power of the entertainment industry is such that we actually sit around and have discussions about World War II or a combat experience based upon Hollywood's image of it. I don't know if it's possible, finally, to replicate the experience of war.

I know it is possible to give us a much clearer and truer picture of combat, but it would be so unpalatable and so disgusting that we would turn our eyes away in horror. The warmakers very desperately don't want us to see those images because it would be very hard to get young men to go to war and very hard to get nations to support a war if we understood the reality of combat.

The Myth of War

War is always about betrayal. Betrayal of the young by the old. Betrayal of idealists by cynics. And, ultimately, betrayal of soldiers by politicians. Because when those young men who have fought in a war come home, they are discarded, left to struggle alone with the demons of war.

This was driven home to me within my own family. My father and most of my uncles fought in World War II. My father came back after the war and hated the military and hated war. He became a Presbyterian minister. One of my uncles, who fought in the South Pacific and was wounded in the war, never recovered physically or emotionally. He couldn't hold down a job. Couldn't hold down a marriage. He was an alcoholic and eventually drank himself to death in a trailer. Now, the case of my uncle who fought "in the good war," part of the "Greatest Generation," was not an anomaly. There were, no doubt, thousands, tens of thousands of families like mine who had to carry this crucible of war in our home, out of sight of the public.

These are the kinds of images that don't propel young men into war, nor do they propel a nation into war. So they are very carefully blocked away from us. We see it with veterans of the Persian Gulf War who suffer from Gulf War Syndrome or suffer from the effects of depleted uranium or from the trauma of being in war.

I read a psychological study that said that being in sustained combat is the psychological equivalent of being in a car crash in which your best friend is killed. These are very, very heavy things to bear. When we see the distress that is unleashed in those who return, we turn away because the myth is so much more enjoyable than the reality. The myth was peddled to us during the war in Iraq by the cable news networks where the coverage of the war existed in essence as a celebration of our incredibly powerful weapons systems and, by extension, our own power.

War is not clean. War is very messy. War is never as tidy as the images of war make it out to be. In fact, war is just pure chaos. The noise itself is deafening, almost unbearable, overloading your senses, along with everything else. You are assaulted in a way that you are completely knocked off balance emotionally, psychologically, and often physically.

We don't want to see and we don't want to hear. We turn our backs on those who come back from war and bear witness to war, and I think this has been true for generations and generations. The reason is because it's so difficult to see, so difficult to look at, so difficult to ingest, and it's so much more enjoyable to ingest the bands playing, the flags waving, and the hero charging up over the hill, which is a lie. It's just not true.

How War Isolates Societies and Hijacks Language

In wartime, the first thing that is hijacked is language, and one never comes out of covering a conflict without realizing that corruption of language is what always leads to war. We turn others linguistically into objects before we turn them quite literally into objects, i.e., corpses.

What happens in warfare is that the state and the media give us the language to articulate the experience we are undergoing. "The War on Terror," you know, "Countdown to Iraq," "Showdown with Iraq," all of these clichés and aphorisms seep their way into our language so that even when we have a kind of disquiet about what's going on, we're trapped because it's those clichés and aphorisms we use in order to try to explain our experience.

You cannot have a war on terror. Terror is a tactic that is employed by groups that often don't have conventional forces behind them. It has been with us since before the Roman Empire. Terror has been part of the human landscape, used by forces under oppression, or forces weaker than the powers they assault, for millennia. Terror is never going to go away.

This kind of a phrase is ingested into our vocabulary and never questioned. It makes it very hard for us to think outside of the box. We are robbed of the words by which we can express alternative points of view. And that's what war does. And you can never have peace until those metaphors and aphorisms that are handed to you by the state are demolished. Otherwise you just speak past each other.

We see that in Bosnia. If you go to Bosnian schools, the history lessons that are taught to Bosnian, Croatian, and Serbian children are not only completely different but are at variance, with each group pinning the blame on the other, historically and in the present. They have no common narrative by which they can communicate. Therefore, they can never have peace. What you have in Bosnia is not peace, but the absence of war.

And this is the strength of the Truth and Reconciliation Commission in South Africa. There, the killers of the South African regime were given an amnesty, but they had to give detailed confessions of the crimes they committed. What it gave black and white South Africans is a new way of speaking, beyond the clichés and aphorisms, by which they could go forward, by which they would not be trapped by their enmity and hatred.

The hijacking of language in wartime is absolutely key to the propagation of the war, and very pernicious to the health and inquiry and self-criticism that are fundamental to creating a peacetime society. In wartime, everybody starts speaking the same way. They call us infidels, we call them barbarians. There's a kind of mirror quality to the languages and attitudes in war, and that's certainly been true since 9/11 in the United States. I was in New York during 9/11, and a few days later, looking at all the cars going down the street with the flags, I thought, "Oh my god, we've all become the Serbs." This kind of patriotic and nationalistic response was one that was deeply familiar to me, that I had seen everywhere around the world. And it frightened me because I recognized that we were all drinking that same dark elixir in gulps that I had seen destroy other societies, such as the Serbian society.

The Cultivated Euphoria of War

When a country prepares for war and goes into war, there is a kind of collective euphoria or madness that takes over the population. I first saw this in Argentina where I was living when the military junta invaded the Falklands. In the lead-up to the war, and it came as a complete surprise, the junta was on the verge of collapse. This was a military government that had been responsible for "disappearing" 30,000 of its own citizens and tremendous corruption driving the economy into the ground. Shortly before the invasion, I was in a huge demonstration that shut down the center of Buenos Aires.

All of my Argentine friends spoke about human rights, democracy, putting those who had carried out the Dirty War on trial. The moment the invasion was announced, it was as if I woke up in Kafka's *Metamorphosis*; I was a giant bug. Any attempt to mention that the Argentine military was not glorious and heroic or that the invasion and occupation of the Falkland Islands was not justified was to court physical violence. And it was a lesson I never forgot.

It has happened in every wartime society I have lived in, including, of course, my own country, following 9/11. What happens is, through war, we feel empowered. We feel noble. We feel great. Blind patriotism or nationalism is ultimately about self-exaltation, and that emotional state is one we don't want questioned.

Those who raise voices of dissent are not challenging simply an idea; they're challenging an emotional state that we don't want challenged because it feels great. The thing about war is that we are invited to suspend individual conscience. And if we're willing to do that, we're embraced in this great crusade. We look around us and all of those people who we were not able to connect with before the war have suddenly become our comrades. There's a sense of equality, a sense of common purpose. We face death as a group, and that makes death a lot easier to bear.

All of these feelings of inclusiveness, which are part of war's illusion of comradeship, are so heady and intoxicating; they free us from the alienation that I think many of us struggle with in the depths of our being in modern society, and for that reason, it becomes very hard to resist the pull. It's why intellectuals are so often willing to put their formidable services to very pernicious causes. It's why Heidegger at the University of Heidelberg would begin his lectures with a Nazi salute.

In some ways, intellectuals are more susceptible to this because they are more on the outside. And those who have the courage to stand up and take a moral stance—Oscar Romero, for instance, the

Salvadoran archbishop who was assassinated—are often not the great intellectuals of a society or even the great social critics. They are those people who have a kind of strength of will and moral certitude and probity that allows them to be very lonely individuals and to say things that in the moment of war are almost tantamount to suicide.

Once you're in a war, you have pity only for your own. We almost become incapable of having pity for the other. Elias Canetti in *Crowds and Power* points out correctly that in war, mythic narrative is so vital and fundamental to pushing a nation into war that it begins with the murder of innocence, with people who have no other real connection to us other than that they come from our tribe, our ethnic group, our nation. Those who were killed in the World Trade Center are held up as martyrs by those who want to prosecute war effectively. That can somehow mean that questioning the war effort is sacrilege to the memory of the innocent dead.

Let's be clear: They were innocent dead. This was a crime against humanity that was committed against us and against those people. But this is true in every conflict. It becomes a struggle on the part of those who speak out against war to make it clear that dissent is not a way of dishonoring soldiers, dishonoring those who have been killed or wounded. The emotional turmoil that is created by the war itself, and the emotional pitch that is created by the warmakers, often quite effectively manages to silence dissenters precisely on those grounds—that somehow what they are doing is criticizing something holy, something sacred, something that no good member of your society has a right to criticize.

Human Nature and War

If you look at human history, war has been part of the human landscape from the beginning. Various people like Will and Ariel Durant have tried to figure out how many years in human history there has not been a war on somewhere. I think they came up with something like 36 years.

I'm not interested in dealing with a world of my own creation. I am interested in dealing with the world as it is, and war is part of our landscape, and always has been, and probably always will be. The difference between wars in modernity and wars of the past is that we are facing those who have the capability to wreak destruction on us in ways that we have not seen before. There was a sort of mutual terror that kept the Soviet Union from launching missiles on us, and us on them. But al Qaeda and these radical Islamic groups have no address. It's not like Iraq; there's no place to go to war. That means the nature of war will change dramatically for the next generation, that my children will face a kind of fear and instability that we have been largely spared.

Now, also looking at human history, we've been immensely privileged. Most people have not been able to live in a zone of opulence and safety such as we have had. But I think that is changing, and it will change our democracy. Fear and the specter of an outside threat are things that those who rule governments can use to obtain greater and greater degrees of power.

Unfortunately, having spent almost 20 years of my life outside the United States, and many of those years in the Middle East, I can tell you that dropping iron fragmentation bombs all over the place only fuels the very elements we should be attempting to demolish. And again this instinctive reaction of fear that you see on a battlefield is one that puts us only in more danger from those forces in our society who do not understand what is arrayed against us and how to fight it.

Societies that define themselves by, or whose great achievement is, military prowess are societies that often are culturally, intellectually, politically hollow on the inside. One thinks of Sparta. It is possible at once to have and build a great military power and actually destroy yourselves from within. One looks at the end of the Roman Empire. The corruption and destruction of political life at the death of the Republic in Rome culminated with the rise of a great military machine, the greatest the world had ever seen. The greatest entertainment industry the world had ever seen. Political discourse was replaced by the spectacle, by the arena.

It's always dangerous to draw analogies with ancient Rome. This was a culture that embraced slavery and infanticide and subjugation of women. Nevertheless, there are parallels that we can learn from. Having a powerful military and diverting public attention from political life with this huge entertainment industry we have created will ultimately impoverish us and weaken us.

What happened in Rome: well, you ended up with Neros and Caligulas. Clownlike figures who would be ludicrous if they weren't so brutal and deadly. We are undergoing a very similar kind of process, where the prejudice against real intellectual activity and real civil discourse and the blind faith in hard military power to the exclusion of all other power will probably end up weakening us and hurting us more than any external threat. In part, that is because we have become so isolated and insulated from the rest of the world that we don't understand how those outside our gates react and think, and therefore we don't know how to respond.

Civilians in Modern War

Most wars are not the conventional kind of wars that we saw in Iraq or that we saw in the Persian Gulf War. Most wars are ethnic conflicts fought between gangs or warlords: irregular, poorly controlled gangs of thugs who have at their disposal a plethora of deadly automatic weapons that they can carry around by the trunk full.

The problem is that these weapons have been so widely produced and disseminated that anyone can get his hands on them. This has certainly served to fuel violence, especially ethnic or tribal violence, in places where the nation state is weak or has broken down.

Civilians in modern war serve as either victims or adjuncts of the war effort. They will man the factories. They will dig the trenches. Civilians become like cattle in wartime. Bounced around, abused, used, even by their own side. The ethnic wars of the 20th century were primarily wars against civilians. There was little fighting between combatants. For instance, in the war in the Balkans, none of the ethnic groups liked the fact that there were people from their ethnic groups living as minorities in territory controlled by opposing ethnic groups. There was a kind of collusion in the ethnic cleansing because all of those nationalist leaders wanted ethnically pure states. In the case of ethnic warfare, civilians are often the ones who are attacked and killed, not because they mount any kind of a threat, but because they come from another ethnic group. Most of the activity resulted in Serbs going into the Drino Valley and driving the Muslims from their homes and dumping their bodies in the Drino.

When I was in southern Iraq during the Shiite uprising after the

Persian Gulf War, there was no clean water. All the water purification plants had been destroyed. I can remember standing in the rain over a mud puddle and drinking this water the color of coffee, which was turning my own guts inside out, and seeing a young woman with her two small children drinking out of the same puddle. I knew what that water had done to me and knew very well what that water would do to these kids. I stood over them and recited in English, not a language anyone around me understood,
W. H. Auden's "Epitaph On A Tyrant":

Perfection of a kind was what he was after
And the poetry he invented was easy to understand.
He knew human folly like the back of his hand
And was greatly interested in armies and fleets.
When he laughed, respectable senators burst with laugher.
And when he cried, the little children died in the streets.

Wilfred Owen, a British soldier-poet during the First World War, died in combat a week before the Armistice in 1918. His story and two of his poems are featured in the documentary film Voices in Wartime.

Dulce et Decorum Est

Wilfred Owen

Bent double, like old beggars under sacks,
Knock-kneed, coughing like hags, we cursed through sludge,
Till on the haunting flares we turned our backs
And towards our distant rest began to trudge.
Men marched asleep. Many had lost their boots
But limped on, blood-shod. All went lame; all blind;
Drunk with fatigue; deaf even to the hoots
Of tired, outstripped Five-Nines that dropped behind.

Gas! Gas! Quick, boys! An ecstasy of fumbling,
Fitting the clumsy helmets just in time;
But someone still was yelling out and stumbling,
And flound'ring like a man in fire or lime . . .
Dim, through the misty panes and thick green light,
As under a green sea, I saw him drowning.
In all my dreams, before my helpless sight,
He plunges at me, guttering, choking, drowning.

If in some smothering dreams you too could pace
Behind the wagon that we flung him in,
And watch the white eyes writhing in his face,
His hanging face, like a devil's sick of sin;
If you could hear, at every jolt, the blood

Come gargling from the froth-corrupted lungs,
Obscene as cancer, bitter as the cud
Of vile, incurable sores on innocent tongues,
My friend, you would not tell with such high zest
To children ardent for some desperate glory,
The old Lie; *Dulce et decorum est*
Pro patria mori.

October 8, 1917-March 1918

~

The Latin saying from a poem by Horace that ends Owen's poem—
"Dulce et decorum est pro patria mori"—was widely understood and
often quoted at the start of the First World War and is translated as: "It is
sweet and right to die for your country."

David Connolly served honorably in Vietnam with the 11th Armored Cavalry Regiment. He takes pride in having been—and continuing to be— a Vietnam Veteran against the War (VVAW). He was born, raised, and still lives in South Boston with his wife, Lisa. He is the father of two grown daughters, Christine and Jennifer, son Jake, and the grandfather of Samantha Anne, Michael, and Aideen, with another one on the way. This narrative was adapted from David Connolly's interview with Rick King for the documentary film Voices in Wartime.

A Soldier's Story

David Connolly

I don't believe that the trauma of combat ever goes away, whether you win or lose the war. I know plenty of World War II vets—the last "good" war, the war we won, the war that saved the whole world—who still wake up nights; my father used to wake up at night. You don't go through things that are that unnatural, that are that unholy, unchanged. You don't lose friends the way people in combat lose friends, and then easily engage more people to become your friend. You're kind of reticent about doing that. You kind of hold part of your heart back.

I think that also spills over to your family life when you come home. You have to work toward being a whole human being. You have to work toward not having that part of your heart—that you had to turn cold in order to survive combat—remain cold.

I think combat also leads to excesses like alcoholism and drug use. Especially in wars like Vietnam, where it was a "dirty" war. It came down to absolutely nothing other than the Vietnamese won. So it's tough to hold onto your humanity. It's tough to hold onto having an open heart to all people after what you've seen and after what's been done to you.

One of the things that VVAW used to teach us is that we're not only agents of the war, we're victims of the war, just like the

Vietnamese, just like those who died. We learn that we should work from the stance that there are people responsible for the carnage that happened in Vietnam, for the atrocities in Vietnam, and I'm one of them. Even though I can say to you I never shot anyone who wasn't under arms and never abused the prisoner, I never committed rape, any of those things, it all happened.

They didn't happen every day. I don't mean to make out the American Army as a bunch of miscreants, because they were not. There was a small minority who were just so embittered by the war, and changed by their training, too, that they came to see the Vietnamese as being less than human. That's how they got all those nice German boys to kill 6 million Jews. The training of dehumanizing your enemy, which still goes on today, it changes you.

What I try to do with my poetry is to distill one second, one minute, ten minutes outside of everything that goes on around you. Just to distill that one little piece of that huge, crazy war in order to point out a specific lesson that I want you to learn. Or just to tell you how this man died for you, for all of us. I want to point out to people just the absolute inhumanity of everything that went on.

I try to write poetry that points out to you the absolute inhumanity of combat. And after working for a long time, it came to this poem, "Food for Thought: 3:00 A.M."

They moved in unison like dancers in a ballet,
the spider 20 inches from my rifle,
the Vietcong 20 feet farther out, inline,
each slowly sliding a leg forward.
I let the man take one more step,
so as not to kill the bug.

What I tried to do there was to give you this vision of looking down my rifle and the feeling of how hard-hearted I was at the time, that I could put this spider's life up above my contemporary. He may have been my enemy, but I'm sure he was a 19-year-old kid, too, you know?

I think that's why poetry lends itself more to issues that you want to be really incisive about, to meet the listener and to try to treat the listener like he's sitting there beside you, like you're looking down the rifle with me.

I don't know if the truth is as important as debunking the myths: Sgt. Rock, and Rambo, who sews his own arm up after a shrapnel wound, and John Wayne. John Wayne wasn't even John Wayne. His name was Marion Morrison, and he fought in seven wars on film and not one minute in a uniform for the U.S. government. Right now we've got a warrior subculture within this country. And these boys, they go off and they are the policemen of the world at the behest of big business, big money, the White House. I think debunking the myths is a real big part of what we have to do.

It's certainly tied up in remembrance and memorial, but it's also people who write about the war. I'm not just talking about combat veterans, I'm talking about people who sit down and write about being physically or sexually abused as a child or an adult. One of the best ways they can get through it is to sit down and open, excise that wound. Let the pus flow. You do that with writing. You do that with standing up and witnessing your own experience. I think it's very valuable in all three things—to hear yourself as a form of remembrance and memorialization.

My poem "Wearing Faces" is debunking the Sgt. Rock myth, where you come in off an operation and don't remember who fell in the last one and don't remember the terrible things you just saw. You don't remember the absolute boredom and the sheer terror even when people weren't dying. And debunking the myth that soldiers don't cry, that men don't cry. Here's "Wearing Faces":

Stand down, guard duty on the bunker line,
Weed-rapping about the last operation.

And someone said; Ya 'memba
That little dude got blown away
In that shitstorm of RPGs?

Then someone cried
And none of us could hold it.

For a while afterwards,
It seemed easier for us
To act like we were men.

I think the tag line in that second poem that some people don't
understand is that it was easier for us to act like we were men. I was
home before I was 20 years old. The vast majority of my comrades
were home before they were 20 years old. The average age of soldiers
in Vietnam was 19 years and a couple of months. The average G.I. in
World War II was 26. That seven years is a huge span of time when
you're 19.

But it was important to debunk the myth that you just carry on,
just suck it up and carry on. That didn't happen. We would sit and
we would memorialize our friends and smoke a joint for them, have
a couple of beers just like anybody would do at an Irish wake—tell
funny stories if you had 'em, cry if you needed to, you know.

To Vietnam and Back

When I left to go to Vietnam, I was hot-to-trot to go. My grandfather
fought with the IRA [Irish Republican Army], and my father was in
World War II; he lost the use of his arm. I grew up listening to these two
men tell their stories about war, one of whom freed his country, the
other one helped to free the world, and I had no idea that I was being
led down the garden path. I had no idea that the country that I was
going to fight for, the government that I was going to fight for in South
Vietnam wasn't a real government. It didn't represent the people. It was
a force cobbled together by us in order to maintain our hold in that area
of the world.

We had no political understanding of that war. We had no historical
understanding of the people of Vietnam—very cursory, if at all. I was
the only man in my training platoon who even knew that the French
had fought there before us. Nobody even knew about the first
Indochinese war. And we were told that we were there to help the

freedom-loving people of South Vietnam, the Democratic government of South Vietnam, the republic. The truth is that I couldn't find those people. The people that I met were all on the other side. Or didn't want to be on a side. They just wanted their rice bowl filled every day and to raise their kids and to live.

As for the Republic of Vietnam, I found out later they had to make up a word in Vietnamese for "republic." The idea itself isn't even contained in the language, it's so foreign to them to live in the type of government that we have, a republic. The longer I was there, the more I realized that we were not going to beat these people; they were just too tough. They had been at war for literally thousands of years without ever being substantially defeated. They'd been knocked down and they'd been occupied, but not defeated.

When I first got there, the Tet Offensive was happening. There were literally communists running all over the place, and I was shocked at first. I remember thinking, "We're going to lose this war. We're going to lose this war." Walter Cronkite was saying the same thing on national TV. I didn't know it at the time. And it got worse from there. Once Tet ended, the nature of the war changed and we went back out into the countryside: the American Army, the U.S. Marine Corps. I contend that we were there to pay the people back for helping the communists stage Tet through the villages.

We began search-and-cordon and search-and-destroy missions. I couldn't help but think of the stories my grandfather used to tell me of how the British army would come through towns on the western shore of Ireland and search them for arms or ammunition or foodstuff, and if they found any of those things, they burned your house. And if they found it in a number of houses, they burned the village.

That's what I did every day in Vietnam. I was only 18 and a dumb grunt, but I'm not stupid. It slapped me in the face that I, in light of my heritage, was on the wrong side; my country was on the wrong side. And, it may sound simplistic that you can't kill for peace, but you can't kill for peace. If you're Vietcong and I kill you, your brother's not going to pick up your weapon and join me.

Very quickly, the loyalty, any legitimacy that you'd give to your actions, came down to your brothers in the squad or your brothers in the platoon, or the guy right next to you. It didn't go beyond that. It wasn't about fighting for the U.S. or Saigon. It was fighting to get you and the guy next to you home. Politics had nothing to do with it.

The first time I came back, on leave, I had come off an ambush patrol at first light and got on a helicopter that took me to Regimental. They cut me orders for a leave. I got back on the same helicopter after it had refueled. It took me to Bien Hoa Air Force Base. I got on a Braniff 707 that took me to McGuire AFB in New Jersey. After a short bus ride to Newark and the hop to Logan, I was standing on my father's front doorstep. I was a sergeant of the United States Army Infantry, but I was only 19 years old. I had no idea what I was supposed to think or say or do. And there was nobody there to help me. There was no decompression. There was no debriefing. At that point, too, in America . . . people were afraid of me.

We had already begun to be demonized in the press as walking time bombs and drug-crazed baby-killers, and nonsense like that. My own family was afraid to wake me up the next morning. My cousin, who I was very close to growing up, came over because she heard I had come home, and she said, "Well, I'm not afraid of him"— and marched right in and woke me up.

When I came back the next time, it was even stranger, because I was done with the war at that point. There was growing antiwar sentiment, but there was also a growing right-wing support for the war, which people like me couldn't understand. I know the myth of the spat-upon Vietnam vet, but I don't believe, really, that it happened at all. If it happened, it happened rarely. I was spat upon by an iron worker, a right-wing iron worker, for protesting the war that I had fought and he didn't.

I really wrapped myself up in trying to raise my family. I already had a daughter, and my writing to try to get my head straight, and protesting the war to try to stop it. I joined Vietnam Veterans Against the War right away. I'm still a member. And I pretty much live my life like that. It's not repentance, you know. It's searching for understanding for me and for you and for America, and to try to stop war as a means of foreign policy.

Once I got to Vietnam and realized that I hadn't walked into what I thought I had walked into, poetry became one of the ways that I tried to sort things out in my head to try to stay sane, to try to make some sense out of what was going on around me. And once I got home, it became even more so. If something woke me up in the middle of the night, some remembrance of a man's death or whatever, I would sit and I'd think about it and I'd write about it. I'd try to almost exorcise the ghost.

To some extent it worked. I really credit my success in treating my own post-traumatic stress to poetry. To try to bring something that was horrible and change it to where it approaches being art, it's very cleansing to the soul, very cleansing to the mind. And I think if you can do that, you not only create something that's better than this terrible remembrance, but you also bring some credit and some justice and some remembrance to these men who died and these things that happened.

And if I can do that with art, fine, great, because I think poetry and art, by and large, will engage you more than just straight political rhetoric. I can tell you what I believe politically. Most people don't want to hear it. But if I can engage you with a piece of art, engage you with a poem that grabs your heart or grabs your mind, I'm way ahead of the game.

Vietnam and Iraq

I started dreaming again. I started having nightmares again in the spring of 2003. I had a friend who was over there, and I knew he was in a very precarious position. He was a platoon leader with 3rd Battalion, 4th Marines. And I guess fear for his safety was the most personal connection that I have for the war. Fear for his safety brought back dreams that I hadn't had in a while. There are dreams that I still have, but, by and large, I don't dream anymore. Not of combat and not of the war. I may dream of the men I was there with, but it's usually sitting around, you know, relaxing.

When September 11 happened, it brought Vietnam back to a lot of my friends very hard, very heavy. And it didn't do that to me. I was horrified by it. I think most Vietnam vets, most veterans—anyone who's seen any kind of conflict like that—were really horrified more than the average American who could look at the picture on TV and see it as *Die Hard 4*.

I have friends over there in Iraq who are my age who are still in the military. And I have friends who are young men, one of whom just got sent back. He already did seven months over there, and they let him come home on compassionate leave while his child was born. And now they've sent him right back again.

By and large, the warfare that I engaged in in Vietnam was running up and down the roads. I was in an Armored Calvary unit, and the majority of the enemy forces that we faced came after us with booby traps and rocket-propelled grenades. That's exactly what's causing the majority of deaths in Iraq right now. And their mission is the same: Ride up that road until somebody shoots at you. And, believe me, I'm not making light of it, but I don't believe that there's any more of a mission planned beyond that. The military is still of the mindset that the way to root out insurgence is to stick men out there, these 19-year-olds, as bait.

And they'll come for them. You can see what's going on every day. It's armored column attacked by rocket-propelled grenades (RPGs). Black Hawk brought down by RPGs. Mortar attacks, booby traps. I was just out at Northshore Community College. I go out there every year and talk with two other Vietnam vets, one of whom was in the 10th Cav, which is the 4th Armored Division, and they have the unit that has sustained the most casualties right now in Iraq. And the casualties they're sustaining are riding the roads and getting RPG'd.

The first Gulf War had those smart bombs and my kids would sit and say, "I can do better than that. It's a pretty good video game, but I can do better than that." But unless you've really had the connection, the experience, I don't think it is as deep-seated. Not that it's going to take me apart. I'm not going to go beat the wife or the dog, or drink myself to death. I'm going to write poetry and I'm going to agitate to stop it, and I'm going to try to influence, not just teach, but influence young men and young women to be smarter about their choices. For a lot of kids in this community, the only way out is the military. But that doesn't mean you have to be a machine gunner, you know. I realize you're a tough guy from South Boston, but I thought I was tough. The Vietcong women taught me I wasn't tough!

Vietnam will always be a part of me, be a part of my psyche. It'll be a part of how I see myself and how I move through the world. Within this community right here, South Boston lost more men per capita than anyplace else in the United States. I knew most of them who died. And that's a part of why Vietnam stays with me. I can't talk about a couple of them without filling up. But that's also why I still do what I do. That's why I write. That's why I try to talk to young men, young women to try to influence them to make better choices. I don't walk around all day saying "Vietnam." There are days when I don't even think about it. But there are days when I think about it a lot, especially when I open the paper and there are nine G.I.s dead in a Black Hawk crash and things like that.

And I'm in schools all the time and I look at these faces of the classes in front of me and I can't help but think, "Okay, where are we gonna lose him? Where are we gonna lose her?" It's an impetus for me to continue what I'm doing. Outside of the art form itself, there's a real political adjunct to this for me.

I, you know, get weepy like a little girl over America, but I don't like the U.S. government too much. They're two completely separate things. I always tell classes when I go in and talk to them, "You're America. God bless America. Watch out for the people in the White House. They do not love you. They do not care for you. To them, you are a number. To them, you are a warm body that they will plug in somewhere to do their bidding."

Not that I'm talking just about the United States government. This is a form of government. They're in the business of government. Again, it's a problem that for a lot of governments, the little guy doesn't count. That's the bottom line, you know? They want to walk their way through the world to keep themselves in business, and what they have to do, they'll do.

It's Not Moon-in-June Poetry

I was down in Georgia about four years ago at North Georgia State College and went into a restaurant for lunch. I had been there about 10 years before that, and the waitress started to recite one of my own poems to me.

And I said, "Boy, I got you, huh?"

And she said, "Oh, yeah. I'll never forget that poem."

And I said, "OK, that's what we should be doing this for."

This was a deliberate effort by me to carry this poem, to carry this message. And the best way I could think of to carry it was to write a rhyming poem: you know, "dah-deet-dah-deet," which I usually do not do. I usually find that intrudes on bringing this point down. If you can do both, more the better. But there's space for it, there are times for it. Poetry, the medium, is going to change by the people who participate in it.

I usually have to explain all of this poem, because even second-generation Irish-Americans don't know their history. Here's "To the Irish-Americans Who Fought the Last War."

In the moans of the dying Vietcong,
from my grandda's tales, the Banshee.
In the calmness of prisoners shot for spite,
the brave James Connolly.
In the hit-and-run of those we fought,
the Flying Columns of the IRA.
In Tet, so unmistakably,
that fateful Easter Day.
In the leaflets found in farmer's huts,
the Proclamation of Pearse.
In all the senseless acts of racist hate,
I felt the growing fears.
In the murder of unarmed peasants
with our modern technology,
we became the hated Black and Tans
and we shamed our ancestry.

The waitress told me that I had ripped that page out of a book that I was reading and said, "You like that? Here." So I gave her the means to study this poem and read it back to me over my bologna sandwich or whatever it was.

My poetry, it's not Moon-in-June poetry. It's not easy stuff to deal with. I hope that I've done a good enough job, that I've thought it out enough, so that it does engage you, so that you do understand the seriousness, you do understand the long-lasting effects, you do understand what we lost—what we lost in Vietnam, what we're losing on the streets of Baghdad every day. I think any writer who writes anything, that is their end: to relay to you what is serious to the writer. But I think with war poetry, with poetry of conflict outside of war, street poetry, it becomes that much more serious to bring across just what the effects are on people, conflict, combat, whatever it is.

Rachel Bentham, *a poet and novelist from Bristol, England, is widely published in the small press. Her stories and dramas are often broadcast on the BBC, and she appears in the documentary film* Voices in Wartime.

War— The Concise Version

Rachel Bentham

contention between people
this is how we begin

specific conflicts
armed hostilities
        the "art of war"
        — it's certainly not a science, is it?
        but doesn't art create?

strategy and tactics
been in the wars?

war baby
war bride
war crime   that which violates
international laws of war
        as if laws are effective
        in wartime.
war cry
war of attrition
war of nerves
war grave

war weary, just hearing the words.

Nguyen Duy was born in 1948 in Dong Ve village, Thanh Hoa province in Vietnam, and now lives in Ho Chi Minh City. He began his career as a writer on the battlefields of Vietnam, and his poetry is suffused with an understanding of love, war, hardship, and suffering. Nguyen read the poem "Fire!" during a 1995 trip to the United States, from a podium shared with U.S. poets who were also veterans of the war in Vietnam.

The Honey Comes from Within

Nguyen Duy

Fire!

1.

We are poets, once each other's match,
our good fortune, we never became enemies.
Tonight we fire our cannons of poetry,
fire into the black night, shells of colorful flowers,
fire into each other, passion without borders,
fire into each other's souls, melodies of kindness.
Fire! Fire! guns of poetry,
thunder! thunder! gunners of words!

2.

Why didn't we live like this when we were young,
when we learn to love each other, we've grown old.
Why was there a time when poetry was dead,
when patches of sky lay in ruins,
limbs lay splattered in blood,
hearts bruised with hatred,
and valleys were traps of tropical death?

Why the time of young men stolen,
the time of young women robbed,
the time of childhood singed in crackling fire?
Our lines lurch like lines of wounded soldiers,
our words stand headless, armless, legless, stirring like red ants.
When will all the wounds heal?

3.

This tear in our poetic soul should not be patched over,
this torn flesh continue to spurt new blood,
pain, hot and fresh, continue to pour on the page,
to remind us of a past,
to remind the world not to play games with blood.
Thunder! Thunder! Gunners of words,
guns of poetry,
pour into the black night shells of colorful flowers!
Fire!

Red Earth—Blue Water

Bombs plowed into the red earth, berry red.
Scorching sunlight burned the noon air like kiln fire.

Bomb-raked funnels turned into rose-water wells,
A noiseless stream of blue water rushing up.

That's our country, isn't it, friend?
The maddening agony, the honey comes from within.

Jonathan Shay, M.D is a psychiatrist for the United States Department of Veterans Affairs in Boston. He treats combat veterans with severe psychological injuries and is the author of Achilles in Vietnam: Combat Trauma and the Undoing of Character, *and* Odysseus in America: Combat Trauma and the Trials of Homecoming. *This narrative was adapted from his interview with Rick King for the film* Voices in Wartime.

The Trauma of War

Jonathan Shay

~

Post-traumatic stress disorder sounds like an illness. It's not an illness; it's an injury. It's a result of something bad that has happened to you. In the case of combat veterans, it is the experience of having people trying to kill you, or witnessing them killing people that you know and care about, as well as the vast array of terrifying and despairing things that happen to people in a long fight.

Post-traumatic stress disorder, as the American Psychiatric Association defines it, is the persistence into civilian life of valid adaptations to combat: the shutting down of emotions that don't immediately serve survival. In a fight, anger is an emotion that is very effective support to fighting for your life. Unfortunately, anger doesn't get shut down. So there is the persistence of anger into civilian life. Willard Waller, a World War I combat veteran, wrote one of the great books on the subject of veterans returning to civilian life, *The Veteran Comes Back*. He says, "The veteran comes home angry." And that is something that we need to remember and have some compassion for because veterans don't like that. They don't like being angry all the time.

Simple post-traumatic stress disorder is like any other war injury. It can be small or enormous or anything in between, but it does not automatically destroy a person's capacity for a good human life. I use a physical analogy that an artillery shell that goes zooming by might take off this part of my little finger on my left hand and I'm right-handed. That is a traumatic amputation, but unless I'm a concert violinist, that's not going to lead to a major disability. I might even cease to notice the absence of that last digit of my little finger very quickly. However, the soldier standing next to me might lose both of his arms right here in the middle of the forearm as that shell that took off my finger goes zooming. A third person might be hit in the head and suffer a permanent brain injury that absolutely devastates his capacity for rehabilitation. He is just permanently deranged, demented from total loss of the capacity for a human life.

Simple post-traumatic stress disorder can have that kind of extreme range, starting with someone who just has some nightmares seasonally and maybe startled reactions. There might be certain emotions that are just difficult for them to reach. Or the person may be unable to go into an open space in a crowd because of the fear of snipers or mortar-men, even though he can rationally tell you that here in the corner there are no mortar-men.

So it can range anywhere from mild to devastating. I've had a patient tell me that at every moment of every day in his peripheral vision he could see scenes from combat. He could bring himself with great effort into the here and now, but sometimes that reality would close in so that no matter how much effort he made, he was in that past reality. When he sat back on the sofa in his living room, he said, "It's like when we were humping the boonies and we got a chance to rest, and I'd lean back on my pack." The past was just constantly there for him.

So the severity matters. The fact is that once the capacity for social trust has been destroyed, once the injury has invaded good character, any possibility of a flourishing human life is lost. Unfortunately, it's one of the most accessible kinds of change that can happen to a combat veteran.

And I emphasize we're talking about a combat veteran. In modern forces in a war, there are usually 10 people in the rear in support capacities for every one who is at the point of spear. So there were 3.1 million veterans who served in and around Vietnam in the whole 10 years of that war.

The Phenomenon Is the Same

"War trauma," "PTSD," "shell shock," and "combat fatigue"—the names have changed, but the phenomena have not. In the Civil War, the neurologists—some of them very wonderful medical scientists —called it "nostalgia." They had some theories that somehow produced that term. In World War I, it was called "shell shock." In World War II, it was called "combat neurosis." And now it's called post-traumatic stress disorder. But it's all the same phenomenon. This isn't something that was invented during the Vietnam War or by Vietnam veterans. It's something that's been with us since the beginning of the human species.

The persistence of these adaptations can actually last a lifetime. They don't always. Most of the time they don't. I don't believe that they are the most destructive and damaging part of what some soldiers come back with. The seriously destructive part in simple PTSD is its persistence. They're unable to get good sleep, because the body is still so keyed up. If you're not getting good sleep, and enough sleep—chronically—everything begins to go to pot. People lose their emotional self-restraint. They lose their social judgment. They're very irritable. It's really bad news not to be able to sleep.

Another thing is the emotional shutting down. If that switch for the tender, softer, sweeter, more nuanced capacities for emotion remains jammed in the "off" position, then negotiating a life with a family, with a sweetheart or a wife, or with children becomes extraordinarily difficult.

Emotion is an essential part of reason. We've all been raised with a kind of folk stoicism that says that reason is over here and emotion is over here, and the less emotion you have, the more reason you have. We've also been taught the same thing about virtue: the more emotion you have, the less virtue you have. Well, it turns out that they're both wrong. Without some degree of emotion, people become moral morons. And someone with no emotions—literally no emotions and no ability for emotions—is incapable of the simplest kind of social conduct that is free of harm to other people.

Trauma in an Individual

The truth is that, except for the Vietnam War, where very good epidemiological work was done, we really don't know how many soldiers from any given war suffer from PTSD. In Vietnam, we can say that of the 750,000 who had high war-zone exposure—that is, those who did get shot at and did shoot at people—about 35 percent met the full diagnostic criteria for post-traumatic stress disorder 20 years later. If you take the whole 3.1 million who were in-country during that period, it's about 16 to 17 percent.

About a third of all people in actual combat will have long-lasting psychological consequences. There are two-thirds who don't, and I can't explain the difference between those who are injured and those who aren't. But even within this broad umbrella of in-combat or not, there are enormous differences in what the experiences are.

I had a patient who was in a platoon of tanks in Vietnam that was knocked out in an ambush within 90 seconds. All five tanks were knocked out. Of the 17 people in the five tanks, only two of them walked away; the rest were either dead or had to be evacuated. Of the two who walked away, let's say, for the sake of argument, that the other guy has no post-traumatic stress disorder today. They were both in the same fight at the same time. Are they the same? I don't know.

What I do know is that about an hour before this ambush, my patient witnessed the platoon commander in the copula of his own tank—for no observable reason—throwing grenades ahead of his tank, one after another. And then he took a splinter from one of these grenades in his upper lip, called in a medivac, and was medivac'd out; he was not there when the ambush took place. My patient subsequently read in the divisional newspaper that he had put himself in for a Bronze Star, for this battle, and had been awarded the Bronze Star for this battle that he wasn't even at. So, did the other person, who walked away and who, according to our hypothetical example does not have PTSD, know these facts about the leader? Is that what makes the difference? I don't know.

The fact is that just as two people who are brother and sister or two brothers in the same family don't have the same experience of growing up in that family, we don't know how to say, "These are the experiences that we have to count, measure, detect, and those are the ones that we can ignore." This is still an area of developing knowledge, and we don't know everything about it.

Clearly, robustness counts. It would be absurd to say that some people aren't more vulnerable to injury than others. You take a stone the size of a golf ball, and you drop it on the shin of an elderly person and that shin breaks. You drop the same stone from the same height on the shin of the circus strong man, and it bounces off without leaving a bruise. So it would be absurd to say that differences in robustness don't matter. Of course they matter, but we don't know exactly how; we don't know the range of tolerance. If you take a two-ton boulder and drop it on the leg of the circus strong man, that leg turns to mush. There are some challenges—some traumas—that nobody is robust enough to survive without injury. And there's a whole vast range of traumas that some people can survive without injuries, and others not.

My message to the military is that cohesion, leadership, and training greatly increase the robustness and resiliency of the troops going into danger. That is the fire in my belly: preventive psychiatry. I want to help the military modify its practices and policies and culture so as to best protect the people that we send into danger to protect us.

The primary prevention of combat trauma is the elimination of the human practice of war. Barring that, the best way to reduce the frequency and severity of injury is to attend to the qualities of our military institutions: keeping people together; expert, ethical, and properly supported leadership; and prolonged, cumulative, and highly realistic training. These three things—cohesion, leadership, and training—are demonstrated protective factors against both physical and psychological casualties because they're combat strength multipliers. My pitch when I talk to military audiences is: Let's help win fights more handily, and you'll be protecting the forces. You'll be protecting their spirit, their soul, their mind.

What Happens to Soldiers in Combat?

A soldier in a fight, especially one that goes on for a period of time, undergoes a series of psychological and physiological adaptations to this situation where people really are trying to kill him. The body and the mind make adaptations for survival.

First, you pay attention. That sharpening of the senses and focus of alertness that people think of as jumpiness, being on edge, nervousness is actually part of the adaptation. Second, you shut down all emotions that do not directly serve survival. You shut down all the sweetness, all the attention to subtleties and gradations of things—unless they happen to be subtleties and gradations that signal an ambush a few steps ahead, such as trampled grass or other signs of disturbance. These two things—alertness and emotional shutdown —are what everyone does who is going to live through a real fight—a fight to the death. We're basically wired to do this.

The deep grief that soldiers experience when their closest comrades have been either severely injured or killed comes from the intensity of the prior bonding that happens to people when they are together in this situation. They have trained together, they have drilled together, and they go into this terrible danger together. That bonding is a phenomenon of nature. It is incredibly intense. In my book *Achilles in Vietnam*, I say that I don't believe that the metaphor of the brotherhood of arms is strong enough. In combat, men become each other's *mothers*. We are talking about a clicking in of some very deep emotional mechanisms that bond soldiers to each other. The grief that a soldier feels when a comrade is killed or severely maimed is akin to the grief of a mother whose child has just been killed. I cannot explain why one mother whose child has been killed can eventually reconnect to other parts of her life and to her other children and why another mother is totally fixated on the child who died and cannot even see the other children she has. Some veterans returning from war appear to be like that mother who cannot even notice the other children in her family.

It is a terrible, terrible experience for the wives, the parents, and the children of the veteran who comes back that way. They usually try to figure out, "What did I do wrong? He doesn't love me anymore." And there are these heartbreaking stories from veterans who have heard their mothers say, "This isn't my son, I don't know who this is, but it's not my son. This is not the same person that I raised." Or, even worse: "Better for you to have died over there than to come back like this . . . " It just twists my guts to even imagine such a thing. And, yet, some veterans with these terrible psychological injuries hear just such words from their close family.

The Betrayal of Trust

Themis is the Homeric word for what's right. If that is betrayed, first of all, it physiologically jacks up the people who've been betrayed. They're in a rage, they can't sleep, they're restless, they're irritable, they're just a mess. There's this enormous desire for revenge, to get payback. If you bring that back to the civilian world, boy, there's real trouble.

If *themis*, or what's right, has been betrayed in a high-enough-stakes situation, you get a destruction of the capacity for social trust. When I say destruction of social trust, I mean not blind naïve childlike trust. I'm talking about the kind where a patient goes into a hospital with a stomach pain and that person expects people at the hospital to hurt him, to exploit him, or to humiliate him. That is a fixed expectation of someone whose capacity for social trust has been destroyed. So, someone who comes back from war with that kind of injury becomes intensely character deformed. Every interaction that person enters into is framed as "I have to strike first." Or "What's your gain, doctor so-and-so? How are you deceiving me by expressing these good intentions?" The injury caused by destruction of social trust and the deformities of character wrecks their lives much more than nightmares, much more than a startled reaction, much more than a shutting down of some emotions, and much more than just being alert to who's on rooftops or between parked cars.

One of the most lurid and dramatic psychological changes that can happen to people in war is for them to totally lose interest in, concern for, or attention to their own safety, and for them to just want to rain down destruction—just kill, kill, kill, destroy. It's not a practical military thing; it's just a personal berserking that seems to leave a physiological imprint that can be triggered again years later, and repeatedly. The word "berserk" comes from the Norse and Icelandic world. It is a state of iciness that I refer to as "burning ice" because of this paradox that it's an emotional coldness and yet a fierce and burning energy. One of my patients described it as feeling like "electricity coming out of the top of my head." And this is a guy who would have blood-pressure spikes when his physiology got aroused this way. People were afraid he was going to stroke out, just boom! The berserk state seems to bring about an irreversible readiness to be triggered, and it can be very dangerous.

The primary group in war assumes this enormous emotional and spiritual importance to the person who is fighting in it. And that isn't necessarily saying that these were all heroes and all wonderful people. People do remember each other's failures and shortcomings, moments of selfishness and cruelty, and everything else. But that primary group is primal and is likely to be remembered as the closest relationships that the veteran will ever experience in his life. Some veterans are continually seeking this closeness, and that in itself is a form of injury.

I have had some e-mail messages from soldiers who are in the Iraq war, or who are back from it. And, these messages are neither worse nor better than those from other wars. There will always be psychological injuries in war just like there are always physical injuries. And the historical record is that they rise and fall together. What spills blood, spills spirit.

How Community Heals Trauma

Narrative is central to recovery from severe trauma. It's not simply the telling of the story; it is the whole social process. The first steps in the communalization of trauma—what I call this process—is to be empowered to tell the story. You have to be empowered to hear and to believe and to remember it. The final step that closes the loop is to retell the story to others. And this is one place where artists have played a role from the beginning of time

The whole cycle of communalization is the telling, the hearing, the leaving and remembering, and then the retelling. The artist can play a role in any one of these steps or in all of them. But it's not necessary for the artist to personally have been the trauma survivor, or to personally witness it. Homer retold the story of the Trojan War hundreds of years after it happened. You need to retell the story in a form so that the person who experienced it says, "Yes, you were listening, you heard at least some of it. And you retold it with the truthfulness, with the emotion, that I can recognize."

The Social Consequences of Trauma

We tend to forget that the fate of most of the human race throughout history and in most parts of the world, even today, is to be ridden down again and again by the four horsemen of the apocalypse. Whether it's famine (related to war, or not), plague or pandemic (related to war or not), or war itself, the normal experience of the human race is to be ridden down by the horsemen of the apocalypse.

The consequences of this are that people shut down. They become numb, they are in it, they're impulsively explosive. The premodern world was not a pretty world, and I'm convinced that a lot of historical mysteries are best solved by understanding the dynamics of trauma.

For instance, the mentality of peasants in medieval times who were continually at war was that of people who were repeatedly traumatized. They couldn't think very well. They didn't have very much spirit, which is to say they were numb, shut down. In countries today such as Liberia, there is a vast amount of psychological and social pathology that is generated by the pathogenic load of the civil wars that have been going on there for decades.

And this is one of the fundamental problems in both modernization, in an economic sense, and democratization in that if you cannot be here in the present, it's very hard to do productive work in the economy. If you cannot believe that the future is real, and that words are at least possibly trustworthy, you cannot engage in democratic process. If you think that every struggle and every conflict is a matter of either kill or be killed, how can you engage an election? It just doesn't compute. I think that there is enormous work to be done in understanding how to rebuild—or build for the first time—the invisible social and psychological substructure of democratic process and of higher level economic activity.

You can't just bring those things into existence by the snap of a finger, especially when they've been destroyed by war or where they've just never existed to begin with because it was a constant tyranny. Tyranny is a state of war. To come from tyranny to a democracy is not something that you just make happen by saying, OK, we're going to have it now.

Sleep and Grief

In ancient war, the fighting was suspended at night. It's only a very recent and a modern thing to be fighting round the clock. There's only one night action in the whole of *The Iliad*, and that's basically a reconnaissance, not really an action. So in the ancient world, people slept at night during war. *The Iliad* gives several examples of truces to both collect the dead and perform the religious rites of cleansing and burying: cremating and burying the cremated remains. As it stands now, there is enormous cultural pressure to just move on, keep on truckin'. Clearly you cannot, in the middle of a firefight, stop to hold a funeral service. I offer as the rule of thumb that if it's safe enough for people to sleep without doing rotating watches, it's safe enough to grieve and that units should grieve as units.

There are some in the military—both line leaders and chaplains—who are working on something called grief leadership, where the commander actually takes the lead in showing that this is the time to mourn and that the deaths of those in his command matter. They matter to him. And some of them are even willing to let other people see them weeping for the dead. In *The Iliad*, everybody weeps. If you ask the question in *The Iliad* "Who weeps?", the answer is everyone. Simple. No discount. Everyone. The love and sacrifice that soldiers bring to their comrades in war is a phenomenon of astounding beauty and preciousness. It is painful that so much love can be mobilized and squandered for often such foolish and venal and wrongheaded reasons by the political leaders who caused the wars to begin with.

I make no hesitation in talking to military audiences, which I do often, in displaying my animosity to the phenomenon of war, and I've discovered that the people in uniform don't love war. I've met plenty of civilians who seem excited by war. They regard it as some grand form of entertainment. But the people who've actually been in war hate it far more than I do.

John Akins enlisted in the Marines in 1967 at age 19, serving as a
marine rifleman in I-Corps near the DMZ and working with platoons
made up of squads of Marines and South Vietnamese troops. In 2000,
he started writing to tell people what violence does to soldiers. His memoir,
Nam au Go Go *(Vineyard Press, New York), came out in spring 2005.
He currently lives with his wife and 18-year-old son near Seattle.*

The Order of War

John Akins

1.

Boot Camp, San Diego, 1967

The herd falls in formation,
learns how to march.
Four lines across,
columns of troops
spaced with precision.
The recruits taper
tall down to short.
Each troop stares into the glare
of a fresh-buzzed head.
Me and other little guys grab ass
at the end of the platoon.
Up and down
the grinder
the back row weaves
a do-si-do.
Our platoon pulls up
at a graduation parade.

The drill instructors command us
to watch platoons that look tight.
Eyes straight ahead,
front rows watch boot Marines strut.
Positioned in back,
we can't see shit.
We eyefuck the area;
a glimmer of chrome
flashes from an officer's jeep.

2.

Vietnam, Quang Tri Province, 1968

Our strung-out column hacks the jungle for days.
Us little guys walk point, at the front of the line.
Maybe your gut steers a route past harm's way.
I move like a teenager seeking his first dance.
My squad leader is anxious to score before dark.
He brushes me aside,
barrels into a burst from an AK.
He goes home early.
I walk point for the duration.
Slip dense tangles, smooth and quiet.
Listen for a click, a rustle, a cough.
Watch for a glint, see a blade move;
toes flex to feel any wire.
Muzzles flash, rounds crack near;
swing right, swing left,
front guys return fire.
Back guys hug the ground.

3.

Vietnam War Memorial, 2001

Now the ranks are tight,
every line spaced even.
Troops form columns in chronological order.
Each troop marks time;
each troop holds position;
each troop stays rigid.
I look for names
in the gleam
of chiseled granite.

Part 2:

VOICES

Emily Warn is a poet, teacher, and activist—and the author of The Novice Insomniac *and three other collections of poetry. The following narrative was adapted from her interview with Rick King for the documentary film* Voices in Wartime.

~

I Trace Your Name Across the Sky

Emily Warn

My father was a paratrooper on D-Day in World War II. Like many men, he arrived back home after the war and was thought of as a war hero. He was Irish Catholic, from Cheyenne, Wyoming, and attended the University of Chicago, where he met my mother. He came from a family of railroad workers, and my mother came from a family of Jewish shopkeepers in Detroit. I think they saw each other as a ticket out of their pasts.

But my father suffered from combat trauma, something that did not have a name then. He drank a lot, fought a lot, was unable to hold down a job. The marriage ended when I was quite young. I always thought of him as a failure who had begun his life with a bright future. He was very handsome, intelligent, athletic, but that war and the effects of it caused him to drink and to die young: at the age of 50. He was walking home from a tavern and died in a snowdrift.

The effect on us was really one of emptiness. He was missing. When they divorced in 1961, my mother packed her three kids in a car and drove across the country to Detroit, where we moved in with her parents, who were orthodox Jewish. My father was never mentioned, he never called, we never spoke to him. He spent most of his life in and out of VA hospitals. He remarried, but that marriage too ended in divorce.

At that time there was no treatment for someone like him, and we just thought of him as someone who had failed in life. Growing up in our family there was a kind of despair and silence and loneliness because of his absence—an emptiness we couldn't fill.

A Reunion at Age 19

I did eventually reunite with my father. My brother was hitchhiking around the country, as people did back then, and he gave my mother an address: Josh Warn, General Delivery, Spokane, Washington. Well, it turned out my father's second wife worked in the post office in Spokane. She attached a note to a letter which said, "If you're Jack Warn's son, contact me." He contacted her and found out where my father was. But I kept my distance. My brother and my sister both went out to Cheyenne, where he had moved back in with his parents. He was on disability. They reconnected with him. But I somehow couldn't.

But when I was 19, at the end of the summer, I went hiking in the Sierra Nevada Mountains, and on my way home to Detroit, we passed right through Cheyenne. I said to the friends I was traveling with, "I'm going to get out in Cheyenne." I got out, and they went on to Detroit. I found a pay phone and called my father's phone number. My grandfather answered—he was 87 at the time. I said, "Is Jack Warn there?" He said, "No, no, who's calling?" I said, "It's Emily. Emily! Emily!" And it was as if I had never left, as if there had not been an entire childhood and life of silence. He said, "Hold on, I'll come get you."

Well, my father had to sober up. So my grandfather drove the few blocks into downtown Cheyenne, and he took me to the Wrangler store and bought me cowboy boots and a hat. Then we went back to the house and I met my father. I was 19, I hadn't seen him since I was 4 or 5, and he burst into tears.

Then all the family came over, and they were telling stories. It was the absolute opposite of my Jewish family in Detroit, where there was a kind of reserve and a quiet. I asked him about the war, and he burst into tears again. I spent three days in Cheyenne, and then he put me on a train back to Detroit. Six months later, he died.

Visiting Normandy 55 Years Later

In 1998, just a few months after my mother died, and many, many years after my father had died, we received a phone call from a veteran of World War II, whose name was Tom Purcella. Unlike my father, he had kept in touch with other D-Day veterans and with the people of Normandy. Every year, he would go back to visit villages in Normandy, and over that time he had collected much war memorabilia. He decided to donate all of it to a museum in a small village in Normandy. One of the pieces of war memorabilia was the cover of Newsweek in 1944, and it showed an American GI holding a wounded French boy. Purcella located the boy, who was by then a retired electrician living in Normandy, and he wanted to find the GI, who was my father.

Tom Purcella told us that the dedication of the memorabilia museum would correspond with the 55th anniversary of D-Day, so my brother and I decided to go. While we were in Normandy, we visited the wounded French boy and his family. And, of course, their being French, we couldn't just visit them; we stayed with them and were hosted by them. We lived with this French family for four days, and went from village to village, where people would take photographs of my brother and this magazine and have him sign it and tell us what they remembered of Normandy. My father went from being a failure in my eyes to being a war hero who had actually liberated the very people that we were meeting and talking to.

I do think that my father was a war hero. I think the evil seemed clearer then than it does now: that it was essential that Hitler be defeated. And my father, along with many many thousands of men, jumped out of airplanes, jumped into the water, and crawled up onto the shore, giving themselves utterly to defeat what was then a real evil in the world.

Going to Normandy, it struck me in a way it never had before: that my father had been banished from my life when we moved into a Jewish community that closed ranks and did not recognize that he had helped save them from Hitler. He suffered the fate of circumstance, of when he was born in history. When these men returned from Europe or the Pacific front, women like my mother fell in love with the hero, with the returning soldier. And she suffered, as many women suffered, a great disappointment when she realized that the heroes were human beings who suffered in a way they had no name for and no treatment to help them recover from their wounds.

So I do think that he was a victim in that we had no way then to help the men who had suffered from the trauma that one experiences in battle. My family's experience did cause me to have strong feelings about invading Iraq. I grew up without a father. He was, in effect, "missing in action." He was a war hero, and then the rest of his life he suffered from being a war hero. So in the poem I wrote called "Skeet Shooting," where I imagine him as vulnerable as a clay pigeon hanging in the Normandy night, I do not wrap it up in saying I redeem my father. All I do is say, "I trace your name across the sky." It's an emptiness, an acknowledgement, in a way, that his life was empty. Now I can move on beyond that emptiness.

American Voices: The Poet in Wartime

Walt Whitman, one of my favorite war poets, wrote very movingly about war because of his compassion for the soldier who is wounded or dying in battle. Now compassion, of course, means suffering with, so he didn't necessarily lionize or glamorize the soldier, but he spoke about [war] in terms that were very real. His beautiful poem "Vigil Strange I Kept on the Field One Night" is about staying up with a very young soldier who died when he was with him. He just sat with him all night until it became light enough that he could bury him. That poem was about how soldiers have to respect the burial rights of their special comrades. So he could write in that poem about digging a grave and wrapping the soldier in a blanket, and at the same time talk about the boy as someone who had felt but could no longer respond to kisses.

Whitman does what the best poets do: He creates a poem, which is just words, and he organizes the words in such a way that they become a felt presence. And when we read that poem we encounter ourselves in it. In his great poem "Leaves of Grass," when he says, "I celebrate myself, I sing myself, what I shall assume you shall assume, and every atom belonging to me that is good, belongs to you," does he mean we literally have his atoms? No. He is making audible a connection between us and other human beings, between us and nature. In "Crossing the Brooklyn Ferry," he says, "For me, the many long gone voices, voices of the interminable prisoners and slaves, voices of the diseased and the despairing, of the thieves and dwarves, voices of the preparation and accretion of cycles, of the threads that connect the stars."

Whitman writes poems with a current moving through them, and that current is one in which there is sympathetic suffering and sympathetic joy. That is one of the functions of poetry. Unlike prose, poetry organizes language so that it approximates music. And because it's rhythmic, and because we then speak it in our own bodies, because we embody the voice of Whitman, we continue this transfer of energy. That's what Muriel Rukeyser called the poem, a transfer of human energy.

There are actually many roles a poet can play in relation to war and many different types of war poems: protest poems, poems of witness, poems of grieving. Poetry has the ability to express and evoke the full range of human emotion, so in part it's just an expression of the range of emotion that men and women feel going to war.

But I think poetry plays a role in terms of healing victims of combat trauma. Psychiatrist Jonathan Shay says that trauma fractures the cohesion of consciousness, and that narrative pieces that back together. But he also says that in order for narrative to be healing, there needs to be a trustworthy listener, and that trustworthy listener is someone who can listen with emotion, who can experience some of the emotion that the soldier is experiencing without doing harm to themselves. Good poems about war, that bear witness to the reality of war, imply a trustworthy listener. They have organized the language both rhythmically and syntactically to evoke those emotions in such a way that one can listen and experience it. So writing poetry, if you're a soldier, could help you heal by knitting together your consciousness.

I think poetry also helps a culture grieve. If we're going to reintegrate into our communities people who have suffered from war, from violence that's so extraordinary that it fractures consciousness, we need in some way to make the grief communal. Poetry can do that. Poetry, unlike prose, has a great deal of silence surrounding it. There are two kinds of silence: There's a kind of silent emptiness I felt growing up—that's a deadness, that's a despair that many sufferers of combat trauma feel—but there's also a silence that's a sense of emptiness in which all things arise and fall away. I think poetry does this in a way that allows us to re-experience trauma without harming ourselves, so that it isn't something that we need to be continually fixated on.

I think this is what combat trauma victims like my father suffer from: They are continually reliving the experience of emptiness or being fractured in hopes of mastering it, but they're continually losing because they have no way to organize something that was the absolute definition of disorder. For some reason, poetry, whether it's war poetry or poetry about anything else, creates an order out of something that was disorderly. But in creating that order, in putting together words in a certain way, you actually unlock consciousness, you can open it up to possibility. That is what to me is the joy of being human, that there are endless possibilities of who we might become as individuals in relation to one another.

Poems about war and grieving don't necessarily end with everyone feeling good, or they don't redeem, or they don't offer some meaning that allows you to go on. What they do is provide you an experience of grief or uncertainty or anxiety that rises up and falls away, so that you know the next time something like that happens, such as a car backfiring, you say, "OK, I'm going to feel this but it'll rise up and fall away."

Skeet Shooting

Clouds hid earth from sky, invisible as you
strapped in a chute, hanging in the Normandy night

until tracer flares, machine guns split the dark.
A clay pigeon had more chance of staying whole.

I listen for the thud of your chute,
collapsing, slapping the ground,

for the thump of your feet, planting
in sodden pastures, boxed in by hedgerows

where German snipers hid. There you stayed,
rooted in fear, though you went on fighting,

drinking, fathering, piecing together shards
into a replica that shattered each time

a car backfired, or a baby wailed.
Your footsteps filled with muddy water.

I fit my sneakers in their shape.
I walk breathing your fear.

I cut a willow branch and trace your name
scrawled across the sky as you fell.

Come Back
Momentary
Father

**Emily
Warn**

California Poppy

I was crying for you.
You brought me a California poppy
in the scented warmth
under the eucalyptus.
You knelt beside me
and let your eyes be my eyes
to the bottom of the earth.
Was that the look we held
that later was no more?
A weight settled in me
as I became the person raised
without you. Come back,
moment in the grass.
Come back momentary father.

Lt. General William Lennox, Jr. *is the superintendent of the United States Military Academy at West Point. He wrote his Ph.D. dissertation on American war poetry. This narrative was adapted from General Lennox's interview with Jonathan King for the documentary film* Voices in Wartime.

~

War Poetry and West Point

Lt. General William Lennox, Jr.

West Point cadets are very interested in war poetry, short stories, and novels because that is their business. Soldiers who have not been in combat always wonder what it is like. These cadets know that they will probably be in combat pretty quickly after they graduate, so they want to get as much information as they possibly can. War poetry, short stories, and novels provide us a way to get that information to them.

For an infantryman who is in combat, it's very hard to articulate what they experience. They go through a whole series of emotions: joy, elation, horror, fear. What genre allows you to portray that better than poetry? I don't know. Poetry can capture all of those emotions at one time and transfer them. That's why poetry is so important. We integrate poetry into the curriculum at West Point, offering a course on war poetry and a writing course.

Now we have veterans: lieutenants, captains, and senior officers coming back in to talk to the cadets. For most soldiers coming out of combat, telling about their experience is very important to them. I think it is also very difficult, and I think that causes some soldiers never to talk about it, which produces a lot of pain. It's our responsibility to talk them through the experiences people have over there, to bring people back to talk to the cadets, and to introduce the cadets to the literature of war so they have a better understanding of what they will be getting into and what they need to know to do the job over there. The literature is always available for us, so we provide it and discuss it in the classroom with combat veterans. It satisfies, a little bit, their desire to know what it's like.

We've had graduates recently, who, after a year of subsequent training, end up in Iraq or Afghanistan. A first captain we had two years ago arrived in Iraq, was given a platoon, and that night was hit. Giving them that kind of exposure to war literature and veterans gets them better prepared to deal with that sort of situation and do very well.

War poetry is a reaction to the situation that the soldier finds himself in. As man confronts combat, a couple of things happen. First, each individual measures the cause against the sacrifice he or she is making. "Why am I here, and is it worth the risk I am going through right now?" I think on many levels it's an awakening for the individual. Second, they are seeing, probably for the first time, their lives passing before them and the threat that they might not be here in the next second, or in the next hour. That's tough. So people confront for the first time their mortality. And that theme comes into play in poetry quite frequently.

How Witnessing War Changes Poetry—and Poets

I particularly like Walt Whitman, because I think Whitman changed when he saw war close up. We all know the Walt Whitman of the earlier days, singing the story of America. I think when he, as a reporter, was visiting his brother [who was wounded fighting in the American Civil War], he saw the horrors of war for the first time. When he went up to the hospital tent and saw the limbs next to the tent where the doctors had been doing amputations, he recoiled. At the beginning of "Drum Taps," he questions whether he can ever write again the way he had been writing. You start seeing the transition he goes through. I think he was trying to reconcile the great "Song of America" with all the terror and the horror that he saw on the battlefield. Ultimately, I think he matured because he went through the process of assimilating those war experiences.

Herman Melville started singing the praises of fighting for an America that was on its millennial track but also started to recoil later. We see some of the same themes in Melville that we see in

Wilfred Owen and some of the World War I British poets, recoiling from what had been an absolutely great progress in technology over the years. Melville, being a sailor, wrote about the sea, but he saw the move from the romantic to "crankin' screws," as he called it, as we put more technology into warfare. I see that trend proceeding throughout American poetry.

The Vietnam War produced soldier poetry where soldiers were trying to make sense of what was going on. Their sense of time was greatly distorted. Most of those soldiers were there for just one year; they knew how much time was left in their tour, and they counted down those days very carefully. Every second counted to them: a day at a time, an hour at a time, a second at a time—this time-counting shows up in much of their war poetry.

Walt Whitman *lived from 1819-1892 and was a groundbreaking U.S. poet, writer, teacher, journalist, and Civil War nurse. He was the author of* Leaves of Grass.

Vigil Strange I Kept on the Field One Night

Walt Whitman

Vigil strange I kept on the field one night:

When you, my son and my comrade, dropt at my side that day.

One look I but gave, which your dear eyes return'd, with a look
I shall never forget.

One touch of your hand to mine, O boy, reach'd up as you lay
on the ground;

Then onward I sped in the battle, the even-contested battle;

Till late in the night reliev'd, to the place at last again I made
my way;

Found you in death so cold, dear comrade—found your body,
son
of responding kisses, (never again on earth responding);

Bared your face in the starlight—curious the scene—cool blew
the moderate night-wind;

Long there and then in vigil I stood, dimly around me the
battlefield spreading;

Vigil wondrous and vigil sweet, there in the fragrant silent night;

But not a tear fell, not even a long-drawn sigh—Long, long I
gazed;

Then on the earth partially reclining, sat by your side, leaning my
chin in my hands;

Passing sweet hours, immortal and mystic hours with you, dear-
est comrade—Not a tear, not a word;

Vigil of silence, love and death—vigil for you my son and my soldier,
As onward silently stars aloft, eastward new ones upward stole;
Vigil final for you, brave boy, (I could not save you, swift was
    your death,
I faithfully loved you and cared for you living—I think we shall
    surely meet again);
Till at latest lingering of the night, indeed just as the dawn appear'd,
My comrade I wrapt in his blanket, envelop'd well his form,
Folded the blanket well, tucking it carefully over head, and carefully
    under feet;
And there and then, and bathed by the rising sun, my son in his
    grave, in his rude-dug grave I deposited;
Ending my vigil strange with that—vigil of night and battlefield dim;
Vigil for boy of responding kisses, (never again on earth responding;)
Vigil for comrade swiftly slain—vigil I never forget, how as day
    brighten'd,
I rose from the chill ground, and folded my soldier well in
    his blanket,
And buried him where he fell.

Paul Mysliwiec *is a U.S. Army First Lieutenant in the First Brigade, Third Infantry Division who led his unit through the invasion and first months of occupation of Iraq in spring 2003. This narrative was adapted from Mysliwiec's interview with Rick King for the film* Voices in Wartime.

I to My Pledged Word Am True

Paul Myslewiec

~

The Third Infantry Division is the army's desert warfare division. In addition, it is the heavy division in the 18th Airborne Corps, which is the rapid deployment corps of the army. We train at the National Training Center in the Mojave Desert, which is much like the desert in Iraq. I was in the Second Battalion, Seventh Infantry Regiment.

As we crossed into Iraq, we saw a lot of destroyed vehicles through our thermal sights. If you saw a destroyed vehicle next to a live one you could tell which was which, but if you saw a destroyed vehicle next to the cold desert you had no way of knowing whether it was live or not. We ended up shooting a lot of destroyed vehicles just to make sure. The first days were bizarre because after the sun came up, we saw they were burned-out hulks.

We didn't get attacked all night. We didn't get attacked all the next day. The next night we rolled out the First Brigade combat team in a column—a massive formation of hundreds of vehicles —200 track vehicles and an extra 200 wheeled vehicles moving through the desert toward our objective. Usually we do everything with either no lights at all or very low lights that can be seen through our night optical devices, we call them NODS. It's difficult to coordinate but it's much safer. The brigade commander made the bold move to go white lights (which is like turning on your brights on the highway) in a brigade column in the middle of Iraq when we're supposed to be at war. It was exhilarating. I thought

we were being attacked every once in a while because I would see
these flashes. Then I realized that people were taking pictures because
it looked so spectacular. It's indescribable. It looked so amazing—a
white lights brigade column moving through Iraq.

The First Big Engagement
and the First Car Bombing

The regular Iraqi Army either capitulated or deserted. They mostly
went home to their grandparents' house or wherever it was safe,
which was fine with us. We don't have anything against them
individually, we just don't want them shooting at us. So we
bypassed them and we got onto Highway 8, which is the only decent
highway in the country, really. It's like Interstate 95, which I drive
to see my parents in New York, except that here we were in track
vehicles. It was that way until we got to as-Samwah, and that's when
we finally started getting into some fights.

My platoon took what I believe to be the first general of the
war, though we didn't get any special credit for that, at the
weapons storage depot at al-Najaf. It was about 24 kilometers
northwest of al-Najaf itself, right after the al-Najaf escarpment. The
escarpment is kind of a miniature cliff that we had to drive up. It
was a 12.5-percent grade, which is no problem if you're in your
Volvo or your Taurus. But when you're in a 33-ton Bradley or a
70-ton Abrams, it's a big deal to have to go up a 12-percent grade. That
would have been a great place for them to attack us, but they didn't.

We rolled up into the weapons storage depot, and we saw a
lot of old hangars. I dismounted and led my platoon around to
look through the hangars. I was the NBC (nuclear, biological, and
chemical) officer for the company, so I was the guy who was on the
ground to determine if there were weapons of mass destruction there
or not. I decided that if there were chemical weapons there, there
would not have been the hideous, horrible swarms of gnats there
that would not leave us alone. So I called up on the radio and said
"Black Six, this is Green One—with all these bugs, I'm sure we're
OK on chemical."

After that we saw that there were admin buildings off to the side.
Whenever you have anything in an army—be it the U.S. Army or the

Iraqi Army—there's going to be paperwork to be done. We saw that there were people coming out of the admin buildings. They looked like they were going to their cars, so I called up on the radio and said that I was breaking off our regular search pattern to go capture these guys. My platoon raced through the desert. We broke down the chain-link fence, just drove right over it. There were all these guys there in their foxholes. There were about 100 guys and they had weapons; they were ready to fight. But as soon as they saw the Bradleys, they were like, "I didn't sign up for this," and they gave up right away. My platoon captured 96 guys, including a general, two majors, and a bunch of other officers.

That was the first big engagement we had, and they didn't fight a lick. Unfortunately, since I was in the first platoon to capture all those people, we became the platoon that had to deal with everybody else's prisoners. They'd call up their battalion and say, "Hey, I have four guys, and I have five guys." They're, like, well, "Bravo 27 already has 100 guys; just toss them in with theirs." So we had to guard everybody's prisoners for a couple days until the engineers were able to make a containment yard and the MPs came up from the rear to take over.

After the weapons depot, we moved up to attack position where we were waiting to go through Karbala. The main thing that was causing us trouble in Karbala was that it is right next to a giant lake. We knew that a dam was holding the lake back, and if the bad guys wanted, they could blow the dam and it would have flooded the entire Karbala Euphrates River valley. That would kill many, many people in Karbala, but we knew Saddam didn't care about killing his own people. If it would keep him in power a week more, we figured he'd do it. So we were waiting there while the Air Force attacked and softened up the Medina division in case we were going to be attacking there. To see what the situation with the dam was, we had engineers analyzing satellite photographs.

From there we moved to a position south of Karbala. That is where the first major car bombing happened. My friend Lieutenant Johnson and four of his guys got killed in a car bombing when a guy in a taxicab had his hood up and motioned like he was having car trouble. When the soldiers went to help him, he detonated a car bomb. When we first heard this, our concern was that the soldiers were bunching up, that the soldiers were doing the wrong thing and they hadn't protected themselves against attack. But we saw the area a couple days later and the crater was enormous. I can't really describe it but it was clear at that point that no matter how far away you had been—if you'd been behind cover or trying to be safe or doing the right thing and properly supervised—no matter what happened that bomb was going to kill a lot of people. We were fortunate that it killed as few as it did. But still, we were very saddened by their loss. We didn't take any prisoners after that, for the most part.

Rage Six, who is actually my current company commander, came on the radio and said on the battlefield update brief the next day, "Listen, I'm sure you guys know, we lost four members of the Rage family yesterday. That's got to bring into focus part of why we're here. It's not only that we're here because the President sent our division here, but we individually are fighting to get our soldiers home as safe as possible. That's the focus."

What that meant to me was that the focus is not staying out of trouble or not having CNN expose you for not doing something by the book. The focus was on getting your guys home by hook or by crook. It kind of put us into a hardball mentality, which worked pretty well, at least for my platoon. We didn't have any casualties. In the company we had very few casualties, even after a lot of heavy conflict from then on in the war.

Adjusting to Urban Warfare

We had heard a lot of things about Karbala. The engineers told us the day before that the lake was too low, that even if they blew the dam it wouldn't flood the valley, so we were ready to attack. The only thing we were worried about then was that we had to go through a very small gap, the Karbala gap, which is a six-kilometer gap between the city of Karbala itself and the lake. We had at least a division to move through a six-kilometer box, which is very narrow. If they were going to strike us with chemicals, that would be where they would want to do it. Another thing we had heard about Karbala was that they had blockaded the outside of the city—not so we couldn't get in (they wanted us in) but so that the civilians in the city couldn't get out. If we had to do any fighting in the city, it would maximize Iraqi civilian casualties. So the First Brigade basically just contained Karbala.

We were on the southwest side and our companies leapfrogged up to guard against enemies in Karbala while the rest of the division and the support troops drove to our west, to go north across the Euphrates River. We had a lot of suicide car bombers—20 or 30 that our company took out. Fuel trucks as well. Third Battalion, Seventh Cavalry Regiment, was moving to the east of us on Highway 9 and were having heavy contact. They had lost two Bradleys and a tank so far by fuel trucks ramming them and then being set on fire. You can't stop an Abram's tank with anything but a direct artillery hit, but you can burn them, because the engines are gas turbines. The Russians learned that the hard way in Afghanistan, and we learned some tough lessons there. So any fuel truck we saw that wasn't driving away from us, we shot. We were going to shoot any car that was coming toward us after they saw us.

Then we moved east into al-Musayyib. Al-Musayyib was the first time that my unit went into an urban area, which was very scary. We saw that there were leaflets distributed around, and they had been translated for us. The leaflets showed a family sitting at home peacefully and said, in Arabic, "Stay in your house, don't drive at night, don't be outside your house near American vehicles. It's very difficult for them to tell if you're a bad guy or not, especially at night. Just stay in your house, and you'll be fine."

We were driving through and we saw people who were in their houses looking at us. It was clear they didn't want us to be there. They were kind of like, "Who are these dorks?" We were invading their territory and their homes, and we were sorry about that and didn't want to be there, but they weren't scared of us. They didn't have the fliers in their hand, but we knew they had seen them. We dropped millions of them. We knew that if they were in their houses and looking at us, they knew we weren't going to hurt them.

The airport was the heaviest engagement of the war for us. It was a quiet night. We were screwing around and then all this goes down: We go after the tanks and all of a sudden my wingman's blown up, and they're OK, but the vehicle is destroyed. Now I'm down to one track out of four. So we're trying to find the enemy, and there are these high walls everywhere and palm trees. We can't really see anything. We're taking sporadic fire. So we sent out the riflemen on skirmish lines to try to find out which walls the bad guys were behind.

When we came back with the Javelins, we were trying to move on to the assault, and all of a sudden this fire truck comes down a highway toward our formation and it doesn't stop. So it gets lit up by two Bradleys and a bunch of riflemen. We haven't yet learned why that fire truck charted our formation. There wasn't a bomb in it or anything, but it was loaded with diesel fuel. If it had gotten into our formation, it could have caused trouble and we were right to shoot.

Then we assaulted the barracks and broke into the wall so we could attack. I led the company assault through the barracks compound. It took a long time, and it was super, super hot because we had our body armor on, which weighs close to 50 pounds. It'll stop bullets—we love it—but it's heavy. Plus, we had on our full chemical suits, which make it 10, 15 degrees hotter. We were absolutely dying from the heat. Then we ran out of water. I went back to my track, and there was no water on the track either because we had filled our canteens with all the water that was in our water cans. We hadn't gotten a water re-supply in two days. At some point, I found one water can, so I strapped it onto my Bradley and went back to try to find my guys.

We had been assaulting the barracks compound through all this brick and all these walls and through this maze of buildings for two hours by that point, and I didn't really know where my guys were. So I drove out, alone, in the middle of the Baghdad airport. I had my GPS and I had a grid to where my squad leader was. I was finally able to break through a couple walls and get to them. When I found him we were overlooking Saddam's palace, and there was this broken water pipe. At first everybody was, like, "I don't know if I should drink this water" but then they realized, "If we're going to die, we're going to die." So we started drinking the water. The first person who drank the water didn't die in 15 minutes, so the whole company started taking water from this one broken pipe that we happened to run over with one of the Bradleys. We drank that water for a couple days.

Whole on the Outside, Destroyed on the Inside

Depleted uranium armor-piercing rounds are very, very hard and very, very dense. So, much like you can stab through your fingernail with a knife but you can't poke through a steel plate with your fingernail, the hardness really matters in a material. Unless you have armor that is depleted uranium, depleted uranium can punch right through it—which means it can pierce any kind of armor available today. Once it gets through the armor, if it goes through a significant amount of armor, the resistance of the armor heats up the round. Whenever metal gets heated up, it starts to spall, which means little pieces of hot metal kind of jump off it as it's passing through.

When you shoot a vehicle with an armor-piercing round, it doesn't do super catastrophic damage to the vehicle. It doesn't blow parts of it all over the place. What it does is it penetrates and then, because of the spall factor, it spews off hot bits of metal inside. Then when it penetrates out the other side, if it's big enough, it will move at a speed that creates a vacuum that can suck bits of people out the other side. If you come upon a vehicle that's been destroyed by armor-piercing rounds, the vehicle will look OK except for little holes in it but the crew will be dead.

Getting hit by any bullet is like if you have an empty soda can and a full soda can that you haven't opened yet. If you shoot the empty soda can, it puts a hole in it and it may knock the soda can over; but it's not a big deal. But when you shoot the full soda can it explodes spectacularly. When the bullet goes through—and it goes through extremely quickly, like faster than the speed of sound—the energy reverberates around inside the can until it's more than it can handle, and the can explodes. When you get shot, because your body is 70 percent water, a very similar thing happens. The bullet enters your body and the shock that radiates out from that, because of the water in your body, disrupts all your cell walls and causes a lot of flesh trauma that you can't see. You look at a guy who has a bullet hole but you can't see all the damage it caused inside. It's that damage and that shock trauma that is what kills people who get shot.

Loyalty and Leadership

As the platoon leader, my loyalty to my guys is pretty much absolute. My company commander is the guy who tells me what to do. He says, "Paul (on the radio it's Green One), you're going to move around to the right to protect Red One's flank while's he's attacking." Or, "You're going to go check out that ADA (air defense artillery)." But what I'm thinking about is: How am I going to array my platoon? How are we going to be able to discern the good guys from the bad guys and how are we going to be able to shoot them? Do we mount or do we dismount?

One of the main challenges for mounted infantry is that you're going to lose guys. You're going to take casualties. That's just the way things are. The better you are, maybe the less you'll lose—or maybe it's just the luckier you are. You don't know. But what you don't want is to get sucker punched. You don't want to get tricked; you don't want to lose a lot of your guys. My riflemen are most vulnerable when they're in the back of the Bradley. You can fit six or even seven, if they don't need to be comfortable. If you get hit by an AT3, AT4, or AT5 Soviet missile and it destroys the track, you're dead and your crew is dead. That's the price you pay, but your guys couldn't do anything about it. They were just waiting for you to let them off so that they could do their job.

Having responsibility for all those guys is an emotional thing. One of the problems is that in the rifle infantry, you can't tell people how you feel. A problem with men the world over is exacerbated here in that it's very tough to describe your feelings. As a 23-year-old two years out of college, you rarely find yourself in charge of 40 grown adults who all have histories and parents who love them and you're leading them into battle. The best you can do is to prepare yourself for that and keep them in the forefront of your mind whenever you do anything.

It's not about your career or not getting in trouble but taking care of those guys who are looking to you—once you tell them where to go or what to do they'll be able to do it. They can execute. But it's not their job to find out whom to attack; it's your job to tell them. That relationship between my finding the priorities and the enemy and then giving soldiers their task to accomplish builds a pretty serious bond. Especially when you get into the peacekeeping side, when it's not the five-battle drills they've been training for since basic training. It's a totally new situation. They are still good at the same things, but they have to apply them differently. They need more guidance—all soldiers, not just my men, not just riflemen. They need guidance on how to use their skills to accomplish this new, different mission. You, as the leader, have to figure that out for them or get guidance or know who to call to get the guidance to be able to tell them the right thing to allow them to be efficient in their new jobs.

The thing about loyalty to the guys is that, in the battle during the war, you have a job that will help them out if you do it the right way. In garrison for a platoon leader, it's not really that way. There's training you can plan or you can do the physical fitness plan, stuff like that, but it doesn't take up a lot of your day. A lot of what you're doing is waiting to train or waiting to go out into the field or even waiting to go to war. The question is: What can you do for your guys during that time? What I was able to do was keep my guys out of trouble with the law. I'm sure you've read "Tommy," by Rudyard Kipling. I don't know that I know what it's all about, but what it means to me is that soldiers are highly underappreciated and poorly treated at home. Then all of a sudden everybody wants to know a soldier or wants to have one in their family or wants to treat them well when the war is going on. "For it's Tommy this, an' Tommy that, an' 'Chuck him out, the brute!' But it's 'Saviour of 'is country' when the guns begin to shoot."

What I spend my time worrying about is getting the correct awards for my men who don't have the background I have—didn't go to prep school, don't have the things to fall back on that I have. So they are by necessity going to put more stock in how well they perform in the army and how well that performance is recognized. They know I recognize that performance; I'm the officer on the ground and I'm able to see how well the soldiers do. I saw how amazing Ronnie Davis is for taking over a fire team in the middle of the war, three days before our attack on the airport, and killing three tanks with Javelins—two with one missile. I'm the guy who saw all that, and I want the army to see that too. So I use that prep school training and I use my University of Virginia education to write well when I write the citations for their awards and try to push those awards up and get them recognized by the army as well—because everyone who knows these guys knows how amazing they are.

What the awards say, for valor or just for service, is that the army recognizes this guy's accomplishments and that everyone who sees them in uniform and sees them with that medal needs to recognize their accomplishments as well. That's what awards are about to me. It's conveying information to other people who just see you on the street and see that you happen to have a certain medal.

It's Just Business

Most people, of course, get to do their jobs all the time. An attorney practices law full time; a doctor is always helping people get healthy. A soldier very rarely gets to actually do his job. We had been training to do our jobs for a very long time, yet except for the squad leaders and the platoon sergeant in my platoon, no one had actually gone to war before. Those guys were in Desert Storm. So my guys were pretty excited to see if everything we had been taught would actually work. Given the confidence we had from various sources, we were more excited than nervous in general.

The first thing that we had to worry about in modern warfare was if it was a good engagement, which is to say if we are supposed to have shot them. Every engagement we had was good, which helped, but it was really more business than anything else. During the fighting part of events it was that they were either threatening us in some way or were uniformed members of the armed forces: We were supposed to shoot them, so we shot them: "Hey, good job, you didn't miss, it was great." It was more of a commentary on gunnery skill than the humanity. Given that we were put there, it wasn't like we were going out and causing harm to people because we wanted to. The more efficiently, the faster, the better aim we had while killing people, more likely the faster we'd get to go home, which is what we wanted to do. So it was more trying to do it well than worrying about the metaphysical aspects of it.

Once we were in the peacekeeping phase, the guys who were causing trouble that we were shooting were the people who were keeping us from going home, because they were the people making it a chaotic area in need of peacekeeping. So, again, there wasn't much, "Oh, the humanity." It was more like: "That dead trouble-maker is one step closer to getting us home." I think the worst I ever felt about shooting someone in the whole war—and I shot both uniformed members of the armed forces and people who were just threatening us—was when I had to shoot a dog one time when we were at the weapons storage depot at al-Najaf.

Now, Iraqis don't seem to keep pets like cats or dogs because for some reason they think it's unclean. Americans, of course, love pets. Because Iraqis don't take care of them and their sanitation is so bad, there are hordes of wild dogs that run around Iraq. Anybody who was in Desert Storm will tell you about it. If a horde of wild dogs comes through, you just need to get off the ground and get on your vehicle, because anything on the ground is going to be eaten by these ravenous beasts. We were about to be attacked by a pack of wild dogs when we were staying at that weapon storage depot guarding those people, so I had to shoot one of the dogs. That's the most emotional I got during the war.

Learning the Hard Way

I don't know what battle is like in general, but I know that a German general, I think it might have been in World War II, once said Americans are so good in battle because battle is chaos and Americans practice it on a daily basis. Germans, of course, are famous for being very orderly and we are not. One thing you learn in airborne operations is that when you drop out of an airplane, you land, find the three guys next to you, and go off toward your objective. You don't have a company formation and then move out in any organized manner. You just march to the sound of the guns and kill everyone who doesn't look like you.

That's what we had. We didn't know where any of the bad guys were when they started shooting at us. We learned the hard way where the tanks were. We gathered the guys that were around us, went, and we killed the tanks. Then we found out where they were attacking the medics, so we went there. Then we gathered the guys who were around us and we assaulted that compound.

The key is that everyone can read a quarterback's playbook and know what the plays are and know who the receiver is supposed to be, but in the middle of a play when things are going all wrong, it takes a real quarterback to pull something out of that and make it work anyway. That's what leadership in the American Army is about. It's about total chaos: You don't know where the bad guys are, and then someone says they found the bad guys. So you gather the guys, make a plan fast, and attack. You make it happen fast enough to be in time and make it planned enough so that you're not just bum-rushing the enemy, which has never been successful. Trying to carve out some little piece of order in the middle of the chaos of battle is what battle is like for the leader on the ground.

We thought that the better we did, the faster we'd be able to go home. On April 14, the company commander pulled us in and said that we were transferring from wartime operations to civil support operations. There was a collective moan from the crowd taking the operations order because it meant that we were then the peacekeeping force. There were a lot of frustrations around knowing when we're going home and then not knowing when we were going home. One time they stopped our mail because they thought we were supposed to go home. Until the week we left we didn't really know when we were going home.

Some of the worst frustrations we had involved the mail taking a long time to get there and not really having a clear mission while we were there. We were still trying to figure out what was going on. In part, that was because we misjudged the Iraqi people and the way they would handle becoming free from Saddam's regime and what that would mean for us. Peacekeeping is tough to make work for anybody. As history has shown us, no one is very good at it. The notion is that America is too cowboy and too gung ho and that when we try to do peacekeeping, it doesn't work. We had the UN try to move in to Iraq and the Americans said, "Hey, we know a lot of security stuff 'cause we've been working in this area for a while. We know how we get attacked. Do you want us to help secure your area?" But the UN said "No, we don't want to be hard like you Americans. We want to be a kinder, gentler peacekeeping force."

Two days later, or however long it was, they got blown up and lost all their guys and pulled out. They're not there now and we are.

America will persevere. Like the President said, we will not tire, we will not falter, we will not fail. We are taking losses—our soldiers are dying over there every day—but they're fighting hard and they're learning from their mistakes and they're not going to quit. That's the key to making it work.

I Destroy Bad Things

I don't really know if I'm a different person now than I was when I went over there. I don't know if it's made me more or less callous, or how it changes the way I view human life in general. But I was always kind of like that, which is part of what drew me to this profession in the first place. You have a lot more trouble with combat trauma in the people who less-deliberately join the army. Now everybody's a volunteer, but some people were coming out of school and didn't really know what to do. The army had a good plan. They joined up. They liked the guys. They stayed in. The guys are great. They continue to stay in. They go to war.

Whereas some other people, and I include myself in the second group, kind of had a vision of themselves that involved military service, involved structure, involved possible combat. That was my job. It was the job I signed up for. I think it certainly affected me less than other people, but it affects everyone. I fully expect to not understand how it's affected me until far later. I mean, I just got back six months ago from Iraq and I'm going to go again. So I'm not done . . . you know; Iraq is not done having its affect on me.

Whether or not adrenaline or an attraction to war were part of what caused me to sign up is an important question. I, of course, can't speak for anyone else and it's a very difficult question to answer, but I think the key is to create good in the world. There are two ways to create net good in the world. One is by creating things that are good and one is by destroying things that are bad. Everyone is different. I have always had more talent at destroying things. So I've been learning to live with that because, of course, it's much more popular to create beautiful things. William Shakespeare, everybody likes him. He created amazing works. It's harder to like people who destroy things, but that's who I am. What I've thought is that if I can find things that need to be destroyed and destroy them, even if it's in a less popular way, I would have contributed to humanity. So that attracts me to war because war is one of the ways I can destroy things that are bad, like Saddam's power base, for instance, with which he completely oppressed and murdered and ran the Iraqi people for so long.

Coming Home

At my homecoming party, I chose to read the first stanza of "A Shropshire Lad" by A. E. Houseman. I read a poem because I followed my father, who is a far more accomplished public speaker than I am and a very tough act to follow, and also partly because I think it's really relevant to not only why I went but also to why I had that party when I came back. At the party was everyone that I had gone to school or college with or knew my parents (who were a pretty high-powered bunch of people), who had all asked, "Why did Paul go to Iraq? He didn't want to go to Iraq, right?"

The poem is about the British Empire. It's about men dying in foreign lands, and it's about appreciating them for the sacrifices that they've made. It's also asking the reader to decide if he's ready to make that same or a similar commitment. I think that was as relevant as anything to why I was in Iraq in the first place. If they understood that poem, they'd understand a lot about me and why they were invited to that party. I thought that that poem more than any other would allow someone to understand why I actually went to Iraq in the first place, which was really the big question.

If I had to describe what that poem was about, it's about continuing to recognize the duty to defend our country that increasingly gets more pleasant to live in. War is not any less pleasant than it has always been, whether you're in a quay and fighting against the Trojans in Troy in 1250 BC, or in the Civil War in the rifle infantry, or you're in Iraq now in the armored cavalry. It's really unpleasant to be at war, and it's always been really unpleasant to be at war. But as America grows—and you saw this with the Roman Empire, too, as it grew—it grows fancier. The Romans started out with very little and then they conquered the Greeks and took all their technology, and then they had the Roman baths and they had women feeding them grapes and they had the Coliseums and it was really great to be a

Roman. But it was still really unpleasant to go on campaign. Fewer and fewer Romans wanted to join the army so they had to go farther and farther outside into the uncivilized lands to find people who still didn't mind fighting. In America, you see the same thing.

War at that time, as well as the French and Indian War, the Revolutionary War, was unpleasant. You get to World War I and now you're starting to see motorcars, you're starting to see electricity. Things like that are coming into the world. War, still totally miserable. World War II, most people have cars, they haven't really gotten into air travel yet but it's started. People have telephones, there's TV; life is really pleasant. They have vacuums to make cleaning the house easier. Everything's easier, except going to war. Now we have the Internet, video games, and Hollywood is making movies all the time, Detroit's making great cars, life is really nice in America. Life is really awesome, unless you're at war.

The farther we progress as a nation and the nicer it is to be an American, the less likely it is that people will want to join the army. You've seen that in the recruitment numbers. We have college funding programs, enlistment bonuses, re-enlistment bonuses trying to make it worth people's while to be in the army, trying to make it worth their while versus how totally spectacularly nice it is to be a civilian.

What A.E. Houseman says to me is no matter how nice it gets to be a civilian, God's not going to be able to save the queen on his own. There are going to be men, and women now, too, who need to put all their own personal enjoyment and their very life on the line to defend all those things the nation gets for itself. You know, they say that eternal vigilance is the price of freedom. That's what that poem means to me.

Kipling's "Tommy" has meant a lot to me even beyond that, even beyond the treatment of soldiers in general by the law or by the cops or whatever. I went to the University of Virginia, which is in the South, south of the Mason-Dixon Line. On Tuesdays, we had our lab and that meant that you needed to wear your uniform all day for every one of your classes—your battle dress uniform. You'd go into a class that you'd only been to on Thursdays previously and people would treat you completely differently. Pretty girls wouldn't sit with you. Everybody kind of looked at you funny. You're the same person but you're in uniform. When you go to your Monday, Wednesday, and Friday classes, you notice you're the same person, and they're more or less the same people. The ones who don't know you are in the army treat you differently. When I had to wake up at six in the morning so I could do PT three times a week, I was not able to stay out as late. The people who stayed out really late would say, "Paul, man, you're really lame. You never stay out drinking very late." I'm, like, "Sorry man. I have to run at 6:30 in the morning." That's hard.

Now that the war started or after September 11 and they know I'm a lieutenant in the army, I get very different treatment. I don't know if that means that I should be really happy that they treat me well now that they know I'm in the army or I should be upset that everybody in the army doesn't get that treatment in peacetime or a combination of the two. But I definitely feel it. "Tommy" is what describes that experience to me.

Why I Went to War

Alan Seeger's poem, "Rendezvous" had a lot of importance to me. I'm not going to say I understand everything about what he's saying, but what it means to me is he'd rather be in bed with his wife or girlfriend. He's not talking about sex. Sex is irrelevant. It's just being in bed with someone you care about. But that's not what he has to do. He has to go to war. He's not going to war with the possibility of death. He's not going to war to be as brave as he can. He simply has a rendezvous with death. One of the ways the poem is important to me is that we all now volunteer for the army. It's not particularly pleasant that we have to go do these things. Now that it's a peacekeeping mission, it's even less pleasant.

Before, when I talked about how we were excited, it was because we were going to actually get to do our job as riflemen. We don't really get to do our job as riflemen when we're there now. When my division re-deploys either later this year or early next year, whenever it does, we're not going to be deploying as riflemen to win a war. We're going to be deploying as stand-in policemen because there aren't enough policemen there to police the population and try to keep the peace there. That's not our job but we're going to do it.

We're going to do it as well as anybody can do it.

The thing about the army that's interesting is that if what is really important to you is getting out of the army, and that's really all that's important to you, you can make it happen. There are ways you can get out of the army. They're pretty foolproof. They just have to be that important to you. They're not that important to me.

I know it's unpleasant to go over there and I know I have to go over there and I know that unpleasantness in general and danger in general is a part of it, but I'm willing to do that. Alan Seeger's poem, "Rendezvous," as well as anything, describes how I feel about my duty to go over there. It's very much that: "I to my pledged word am true. I shall not fail that rendezvous."

I think it's absolutely critical that we have a professional army. In the 4th century BC, the very first professional army in the world conquered the entire known world. Alexander the Great, led the first professional army ever. Before that it was what we refer to as "weekend warriors." A professional force that trains year-round is essential to be able to have that coordination—no matter what the mission is. If you've done other missions with the same unit, you know how to coordinate, how to plan, and how to act with that unit, and you're going to be more successful in anything you do. Furthermore, when you go into battle, you want to know that the guys to your left and right aren't there because someone forced them. You want to know that as little as you want to be there, they want to be there, even if for different reasons; they signed up and volunteered the same way you did. They didn't get stuck there because the judge said that they had to go to prison for 10 years or go to Iraq. Some of those guys were great in Vietnam and some of those guys were great before, but it gives soldiers now a lot of confidence to know that the men and women they go into battle with are volunteers just like they are.

Alan Seeger *had barely passed his 28th birthday when, during the First World War, he charged up to the German trenches on the field of Belloy-en-Santerre and got caught in a deadly flurry of machine-gun fire. He fell, with most of his comrades. Lines from his poem "I Have a Rendezvous with Death" are recited by 1st Lt. Paul Mysliwiec in the documentary film* Voices in Wartime.

I Have a Rendezvous with Death

Alan Seeger

I have a rendezvous with Death
At some disputed barricade,
When Spring comes back with rustling shade
And apple-blossoms fill the air—
I have a rendezvous with Death
When Spring brings back blue days and fair.

It may be he shall take my hand
And lead me into his dark land
And close my eyes and quench my breath—
It may be I shall pass him still.
I have a rendezvous with Death
On some scarred slope of battered hill,
When Spring comes round again this year
And the first meadow-flowers appear.

God knows 'twere better to be deep
Pillowed in silk and scented down,
Where Love throbs out in blissful sleep,

Pulse nigh to pulse, and breath to breath,
Where hushed awakenings are dear:
But I've a rendezvous with Death
At midnight in some flaming town,
When Spring trips north again this year,
And I to my pledged word am true,
I shall not fail that rendezvous.

Craig White, NBC cameraman, was embedded with the 3rd Infantry Division, one of the first U.S. Army units to enter Baghdad in April 2003. The following narrative was adapted from White's interview with Rick King in the documentary film Voices in Wartime.

Combat Is a One-way Door

Craig White

I'd been to Baghdad the year before the war, and witnessed a very silent population of people who were very repressed—more silent than I'd ever seen anywhere in the world. It was pretty obvious they were in a brutal dictatorship. They were afraid to say anything. They were always looking over their shoulder.

My next time in Iraq was the beginning of the war, but before that I spent some time in Kuwait with the correspondent David Bloom contemplating the question of how we cover a war. We could do it from a distance, but then you never really see war. The only way to really experience it, see it, report on it, is up close. So we found out how to use modern technology to do that and decided to do it. We wouldn't take the risk of doing it from the Iraqi side. We did it from the American side. To do it from the Iraqi side would have been really close to suicide.

I was embedded with the Third Infantry Division of the army. It was what they call heavy infantry, meaning tanks and heavy fighting vehicles. It was the oft-used tip of the spear. We were some of the first people to go into Iraq.

The beginning of the war was much as a travelogue. There was not that much fighting that we saw. It was kind of strange; we went in late on the night of March 19, when the army crossed the berm into Iraq. I never saw too much resistance. People from Iraq welcomed us with open arms, cheering.

Next we traveled for hundreds of miles through this bleak desert and emerged very close to Baghdad. We got into some fighting in some small towns that reminded me of Vietnam. It was ironic—I could have had a picture that would have definitely made it on the front page of the *Los Angeles Times*, *Washington Post*, or *New York Times*. (This was about a week into the war, when the "shock and awe" was not going all that well.) One of the tanks ahead of us in a column slid into a canal and stopped us dead. Over there all the tanks have names. This one was called "Bush and Company" and I had a picture of it.

Video Game Warfare

I expected that we'd be fighting war in the desert, and that's how it started. Tanks would be far in the distance. I had special cameras brought for us that could show things a mile away, and it looked like a video game. You'd see a tank, a little poof! You'd see in the distance another object go poof. It was just like a video game. There was no cause and effect at that point. Somebody pushes a button, that tank shell goes away, and something explodes off in the distance. And someone, through a long lens, sees that something's hit, and off they go to identify the next threat and kill it. That's what soldiers are trained to do.

And desert warfare is a long-distance war. The army put up what they call a wall of steel. They start at great distances with rockets, cruise missiles, and airplanes, and then it becomes artillery, and then it becomes tanks and then it becomes Bradley fighting vehicles, then machine guns and rocket launchers. Then, if necessary, it gets down to soldiers coming out of the back of those and fighting in trenches, close up with other soldiers.

It was no contest, at first. The Americans basically just rolled over what was in sight. There was very little resistance. Very often, Iraqi soldiers chose to leave a uniform—usually a new one—a brand-new pair of boots, a rifle, and a helmet, and that's all we would see. They chose not to fight. They were told by Americans, through whatever means, that if they went to their garrisons and didn't fight, they wouldn't be killed. Some chose to do that. I think it was only the nonuniformed, nonregular fighters who chose to fight.

Entering Baghdad

Around April 4, we crossed the Euphrates River for the first time, which meant we were very close to Baghdad. At that point there were still Iraqi tanks, most of them disorganized, some trying to flee, some looking for targets and not knowing where they were going. One at a time they were being destroyed and the people in them killed by American tanks over the course of several days. Then, the Americans got involved in a propaganda war to a certain extent. The first soldiers to enter Baghdad did what they call a "Thunder Run:" They took armored vehicles, ran 'em right through part of Baghdad and captured the airport. The Iraqis turned that around to say that the Americans came into their city, and they were repelled. Our military took great offense at that, and they made a bold move on April 7 to go right into the heart of Baghdad. Originally everyone else thought that they would circle the city and there'd be some sort of siege of the city, very reminiscent of a Sarajevo or a Stalingrad, but that didn't happen. They went right into the city, cutting it in half, and seizing the palaces and all the important government buildings in one day.

But that meant they had to take a big chance with American lives. It's a chance that ultimately paid off for them, but it came very close to not happening. When America was watching statues fall, palaces being destroyed, and jubilant Iraqis, American soldiers were fighting a hard battle for three days that could have gone either way. They made a choice: If they couldn't secure a way out within eight hours, they were going to turn around and leave. Eight hours came, eight hours went, and it was very unclear whether they would make it. A colonel made a choice to stay, took a chance, and it paid off for the Americans.

Seven Hours Under Fire

The battalion I was with had three objectives: three key intersections on a road. The objectives were called "Moe," "Larry," and "Curly"— the Three Stooges. I was at Curly with about 80 American soldiers. We knew it would be a bad day going in there, that all of these vehicles would take fire. People started taking clothing out, smart people started bringing more ammo in. I saw soldiers taking rings off, letters to home—possible last letters home being put in envelopes and sealed—and in we went.

Immediately as they entered the city, they started taking fire from both sides. We thought it was the Iraqis who were waiting for us, but it was actually Syrians. Ahead of us they went on to Moe and Larry; while we stayed at Curly, which was supposed to be lightly defended. I was mainly with mechanics, people who weren't necessarily trained for this sort of thing. We thought we'd be in the rear of the fighting. But as it turned out, we were probably in the most heavily defended place, and we were under a bridge under fire probably for about seven hours.

About six hours into it, it looked like we were starting to run out of fuel and ammunition. People were wounded on both sides. It was closer war—not hand-to-hand, but you could see your enemy. It never really hit me until then that most of these soldiers had never been fired at before in their lives. And for the first time 18-, 19-year-old boys became men in many ways. They had some hard choices to make. I saw people grow up very quickly; I saw people who were expected to do very well decide not to come out of a vehicle. The medics certainly weren't expecting to be in a place like that. We started taking some fire from mortars and RPGs, and there was constant small arms fire.

Special Forces people came in with an attitude and thought they were pretty hot with their baseball caps turned backward, a swagger to them. They lasted a few minutes. They went into a situation to try and clear out an area underneath a bridge where we were, and two of them got hit right away. The first guy was really bad—it looked like he was going to lose a leg. It turned out that he did. So they got out of there.

They decided to bring in a resupply convoy of fuel and ammo trucks for the tanks, for the Bradley fighting vehicles, for small arms, and a bunch of mechanics—it was literally the cavalry coming, we thought. On the way in, they ran a gauntlet of rocket-propelled grenade fire, machine-gun fire. Two soldiers were killed. One had his head blown off; the other one had a big hole in his side. One guy was actually blown right out of his vehicle. The other one pretty much was killed and splattered over the rest of the people that were in his truck. By the time they got to where we were, several of those trucks were on fire. Then they started to get hit again with RPG fire, so we were now all hunkered down together. We were surrounded. Fire was coming from all sorts of directions, we couldn't get any kind of air cover because it was a smoky day. We all thought, "We might not make it out of here."

As these trucks were on fire, I watched soldiers make choices that I probably couldn't have made. I saw soldiers running into these burning trucks full of ammunition popping off. There was depleted uranium, and radiation going up into the air everywhere. People were actually running into these burning trucks, trying to save them. The chaplain we were with, Steve Hummel, made a choice. He was a former infantryman before he became a chaplain. He chose to pick up his automatic rifle and fire back.

We were lucky. There was one rifle left, standing by itself. It was a sniper rifle, not exactly what someone would use in a case like that. It was the only weapon that I could see, and we all thought "we're gonna get overrun." We took some hard artillery shots near us, and it looked like the people around us sort of had our number.

And I say "our," because I was with them, but I very much separate myself from them. I'm not a combatant. I came very close to becoming one to save my own life, and I would have used that sniper rifle, if I had had to. We'd all heard stories about what had happened down south. I was not under any illusion that because it said "Press" on my flak jacket that I would be treated differently from any other soldier. Soldiers had been executed there, some taken as prisoners of war. And I had made the decision, this time, that I would probably not just be taken prisoner, just put up my hands. I would probably fire back for the first time in my life. I'm not a gun person, by any stretch of the imagination.

It Was Literally the Fog of War

Combat under that bridge was the loudest thing I'd ever heard in my life. I'd lost hearing in my right ear to a machine gun back in 1980. My ear's been ringing since then. That's why I wear earplugs whenever I'm around something loud—I was wearing earplugs that day, but it was so loud. Every time a large shell would go off, you'd reflexively open your mouth from the concussion. I was very close to a 50-caliber machine gun, it's just incredible how loud it is. You can't see very well, the smoke is stinging your eyes as it drifts back and forth. What you see and what you don't see changes from one moment to another. It is literally the fog of war. In the middle of all this, people firing from all directions: RPGs were coming in, machine-gun fire, and someone yelled "Technical!"

The first time I ever heard the term "technical" used was in Somalia, places where people would take a Toyota pickup truck or a van and mount a machine gun on it. This truck van came screaming at us over an overpass in the middle of this at high speed. Immediately guns swung over and started shooting, and they destroyed it within a matter of 4 to 5 seconds. Only then did they realize that it probably wasn't a combatant; it was just someone trying to get out of there.

In the next two days, I saw that happen a number of times: Innocent families who were trying to flee to a safer place would get caught in the middle of a battle, and they always lost. They always got blown up. It was rare that people would stop when warning shots were fired. You'd think that they would stop, but people don't know; people are scared and they got destroyed. It's difficult to see people burning inside of a vehicle, or in one case to see an adult and a small person—probably a child—coming out the back of a car on fire. Those are all hard, hard things for soldiers to see and for anyone to witness.

There was a major and his group of people who came in, and for the first time ever they were going to try to give psychological counseling to soldiers right after combat, first time ever. And because I was close to a lot of these soldiers, or they trusted me, I was able to go in and shoot that, and it was amazing at what bothered them the most. Besides seeing their own comrades killed and dead, the incidents where they had mistakenly killed or injured innocent citizens just weighed on them so heavily, and my guess, it'll weigh on them the rest of their lives. It's very very difficult to know you may have pulled a trigger or thrown a grenade at some innocent person. In one case, they had a woman who survived one of those attacks. She was in the back of a car, and her husband and son were killed in the front seat. For two hours afterward, she sat there, she could speak English, and kept going to their faces saying, "Why? Why did you kill them? Why did you shoot?" And most of them said that they were dreaming of that, having nightmares over and over and over again.

After we'd been in battle for about six hours, there was a feeling— I've been in crowds and felt it—there's an electricity, something changes in a second from people being confident to people going "Oh my God, we're not going to make it." And that's the sense that I had. As it started getting heavier and faster and coming from different directions, it felt like the Americans were not in control of the situation and that it didn't look that we'd survive.

Two American soldiers trying to bring in supplies for us were killed, one blown out of a vehicle, his body left there, and the other one —I remember them bringing what was left of him on a stretcher. I tried to shoot it in such a way that you didn't see the fact that his head was pretty much blown off, but you could tell it was a dead American there. They brought him to where we were: a medical group that we were with who were trying to patch up soldiers that were shot. At the same time, I watched American soldiers wading into this and pulling out enemy combatants and treating them along side American combatants.

After our relief convoy got to Curly, and the Iraqis and Syrians who were there started blowing it up, we knew we had to get out of there. We had large tank weapons blowing up everywhere in trucks around us, and we decided get out as fast as possible. We ran. We left a few vehicles here to hold the intersection and ran to the next intersection as fast as possible, shooting and being shot at the whole way. It was running another gauntlet to get to the next place of relative safety underneath a bridge that was built by Germans. Thank goodness it was because it was built very well and withstood a lot of pounding that would not necessarily have happened in the Third World. So here I was in Iraq being saved by a German bridge while being with the American soldiers. It's just part of the absurdity of war.

One of the most amazing pictures I saw was of an American soldier on a stretcher being carried out with a bullet in his knee. Ironically, we found out it was an American bullet. He had a shotgun on his lap protecting the people who were carrying him out on a stretcher, and you actually could see him turn over while on the stretcher and shoot and kill a man. It was pretty amazing to see that.

I'm trying to think what else. People running into the trucks, I think I mentioned that. There's a few things like that. Bob Gallagher, a veteran of several wars. He was in Grenada, he was in Panama, he was in Mogadishu. He was the guy who while he was being bandaged up was still firing. He got his fourth Purple Heart that day, the day I was with him.

But it's not all craziness like that. There are absurd moments in the middle of a gun battle where people are not sure if they are going to live or die. I saw a sergeant who was firing, and every 100 rounds, he had to go down into his armored vehicle and pull up another box and put it on to fire again. One time he went down there, and he was down too long. I thought he might have been hit. What happened? He opened the door of his armored vehicle and a pot of coffee and mugs came out. These guys are so dead; they've been awake for so long. They needed the caffeine. These guys are doing what they do, having coffee. That's an absurd moment in the middle of a war.

I was at Larry for about two days. During that time all sorts of combatants just seemed to keep coming at us—mainly in buses, trucks, and cars. I remember a car-bomb coming at us and a lot of shooting. It got really close and Boom! blew up. Huge fireball. My camera only got the beginning part of the fireball. Then it shut off from the concussion. I remember being thrown backward and couldn't find my camera. It was probably 60 or 70 feet behind me in the rubble. Took me an hour to find it.

No Rest for the Weary

I learned a lot about sleep or lack thereof during this war. I think the army—categorically, I can say—does not plan for sleep. They don't plan to let soldiers sleep. We would go 72-hour stretches with no sleep. I saw soldiers having to fall asleep in a long convoy of 8,000 vehicles that would stop and go, stop and go. People would fall asleep, there'd be people knocking on the door trying to wake them up, to keep them going.

I entered combat in a situation where I'd had maybe an hour's worth of sleep in the last 48 hours. I've also been in a situation where I've seen everybody fall asleep, with the guns, in a combat situation, just totally exhausted. Bad decisions can be made, obviously, because of fatigue, and I have no doubt that that happens. I saw it happen a couple of times. In wartime, life-and-death decisions are made in the snap of a finger—they have to be. Some are made right, some are made wrong. People rely on their training, they go back to automatic pilot whenever possible, but they have to make decisions based on information, and information may not be there. Things happen at long distance in war now, with weapons things can happen from a quarter mile away or a mile away. But how do people really know what it is they're shooting at? They make assumptions. We all read into what we see.

I'm sure a lot of people would like those decisions back. It's the nature of war that mistakes will be made, innocent people will be killed, your own people will be killed. That happens more than we know. There is so much metal in the air in modern warfare, infantry-type fighting that Americans get killed all the time. It's one of the other things that soldiers have to deal with for the rest of their lives—the idea they may have pulled the trigger that killed one of their own.

The most common mistake that people make when they call for artillery support in a fire situation is to give their own grid coordinates. They have systems now to try to stop that from happening, but time and time again people have done that—called in artillery right on their head. And in a battle situation there've been times when you have to call in artillery support in something called "danger close," which means the enemy is so close to me that if you make a mistake, I die.

That's stress—knowing that you're calling in weapons for someone who's so close to you that if they're off a little bit, you die and so does everybody around you. It's difficult to be a soldier—that's one thing I've learned specifically in this one. I think it's one of the hardest jobs in the world. I don't think that people ever can appreciate what people do in the military—and how underappreciated they are and how abused they are by our society. I saw it this time, I've seen it before, but this was the worst.

People Explode

In modern warfare, as I saw in Iraq, people don't die like they do in television or the movies. You don't see people get hit with a weapon, have a big red spot and fall down. People explode. Arms come off. Heads come off. Torsos are severed. They just explode. It's devastating to watch the first time you see it; it's like someone punches you. When I think about it, the army was totally unprepared for the kind of warfare they would find—not warfare, but policing—that they would find in Iraq after the war. There were times when people would be in what they call a paladin, a battle king; this is a moving howitzer, 155- or 105-millimeter canon on top of a vehicle that's supposed to patrol streets. The only thing they could do with that weapon would be to blow up a whole building.

I think combat is a one-way door. When someone is in that and witnesses it and participates in it, especially, I think you never come back. I don't think you possibly can. You're altered. I've definitely been altered by what I've seen. Changed. My priorities in life are different. It's obviously the most horrible thing people can imagine. There's no glory in it. The most adamantly antiwar people I know really are people who've been there, done that, don't ever want to do it again. I spoke with a woman recently who was talking about her husband who's a soldier, and she said: "GI Joe went to Iraq, and somebody else came back."

I think of myself as a reliable eyewitness, I'm trained to be that, to try to be objective, and yet I don't necessarily trust my memory in some cases. I woke up one night underneath a 50-caliber machine gun firing. I didn't wake up on the first shell—and these are very, very loud and there were hot shells coming down on my face—I didn't wake up on the tenth. It was probably 30 shots in before I woke up and immediately looked out into the darkness: flames, things happening, and I'm not sure where the dream left off and reality started. That's a very, very disconcerting thing.

When I was under that bridge in Iraq, besides thinking of "Wow, I really got myself into it this time, how stupid this is, how crazy it is," what I was experiencing was very strange. At one point I thought I was in Lebanon. It was so familiar that I was sure for a period of time—maybe 15 seconds, 30 seconds—that I was in Lebanon. Nothing is like it in the world.

In war, you live for the moment. You live for what's happening immediately around you. Your senses are heightened; you're in a fight-or-flight situation that you're trying to desperately control. There have been quite a few times when I thought, "I have to run," but where are you going to run to? And that clouds things in terms of judgment. People care about the people immediately around them. That seems to be what counts most—I think that's why most soldiers fight, not for the greater cause but for the guy next to him. It's not what people think—it's not raw patriotism, because in a war situation, almost everybody's scared. The level of fear kind of rises and falls like a tide in people. I'm sure everyone in a situation like that thinks, "What am I doing here? Why am I here? Oh my God, I made the biggest mistake of my life. How did I get myself into this?" But I think that's a common feeling to a lot of people.

I don't know what is worse: somebody being too brave, or somebody being paralyzed by fear. They're both very bad. Sometimes people take stupid chances, and sometimes people can't function or just run. Either one will kill you in a war. I watched a man run out in front of a tank. I'm not sure what his rank was. He tried to try to draw the fire of a tank at him, because he knew that the tank was aimed at some of his comrades in a trench, and it would probably kill them. That takes a lot of bravery. It's also crazy. It depends on how you look at it. He could have died.

War is so arbitrary and capricious. You could be three feet away and live or die. Soldiers in war wonder over and over: "Why did I live? Why did he die?" There's a lot of survivor's guilt. I have no doubt that the price that our military and our country will pay is a lot higher psychologically. With combatants, post-traumatic stress disorder is much higher than we'll ever know. I feel part of it myself, I've gone through some therapy. I participated in group therapy with some of my comrades. I think everybody who really saw a lot, or experienced a lot, benefits from something like that. One of my colleagues around the table was saying, "I can handle this. I've covered 28 wars. I can survive in war; it's the one thing in life I can do." I remember looking at him and saying, "Bullshit. You can't tell me that you don't wake up in the middle of the night in a cold sweat, living through this over and over again, the same things, over and over again." And he looked at me and said, "Well, I'm not saying that doesn't happen. You know, I go out with the guys, I get drunk, I've hit the bottle, I've had two nervous breakdowns, but I can handle it."

That denial is fairly prevalent. You see it with the people that I work with around the world. I see the same newspeople, it seems, who want to do it over and over again. That's pretty bad seduction; it really is. I don't know why people choose to do this over and over again. I don't know how I can. I'm not sure. At some point you have to call it quits and walk away from it. There's a certain exhilaration in surviving. The first couple times, there's a huge adrenaline rush in saying, "Wow, that was horrible, and I'm alive." That is followed usually, by the horror of it. The next time, it doesn't happen like that. The time after that, it happens even less, and the exhilaration of living through something doesn't happen at all after a while. You just dread.

I remember interviewing a young infantryman who stood out because he was skinny and kind of meek. I think he was 18 years old and from the Midwest. After talking with him, I remember he looked a little scared, and he was all wrapped up in his flak jacket with grenades hanging from him and ammo everywhere. He seemed too small for what he was carrying. I said, "Why are you in the military? Why aren't you going to college?" And he looked at me and said, "Mister, I wasn't mature enough to go to college." The irony of that was amazing: Here's somebody who thinks they're not mature enough to go to college. Obviously he was told that by somebody and is now in a position to take lives and make very weighty decisions. It's amazing. And I saw so many people like that.

I ran into that gentleman in group therapy about five weeks later, and he was a very changed individual. His body language was different. We were in Baghdad. The fighting had stopped. He had to have his weapon there, and you could see that nervousness that soldiers have, of having a weapon. It's training, but a lot of it's a security blanket. He was wide-eyed, mistrusting, and mad at everybody around him, including his own officers. He couldn't get a sentence out without saying "Fuck" twice. He was a different person from being this meek, young kid.

I don't think young soldiers really know for a long time what happens to them. They know the specifics of nightmares. They know that they don't want to do it again, but I don't think they really know the long-term effects of war on them. People tend to close up or lie. You hear a lot of bravado afterwards. A lot of that is not telling what they really did or felt. A lot of that is being trained to be a male, to not acknowledge the intense fear, and wanting to have some value. They tend to swagger. Deep down inside, it's not that way at all. There's a depression.

Embedded Reporters

The situation I was in was good. The soldiers and commanders gave us free rein. We could go where we wanted to go and cover what we wanted to cover.

I was never in a situation where I had to report on the military doing horrible things: especially premeditated horrible things, which didn't happen. They generally conducted themselves in an extremely professional way.

On the other hand, I had to guard myself against a Stockholm Syndrome. That is, you're living with people and you get to know them. You see pictures of their children and learn about their family situations. They're providing you with some relative safety: they're guarding you. They're giving you food and a place to sleep. There's a natural reaction in a situation like that to give them the benefit of the doubt, so I had to constantly rethink everything and try to get back to a neutral stance. I think I was fairly successful at doing that, but I can't say I was 100 percent successful.

A lot of people I saw were cheerleaders. And I know people who were not given access to anything. In some cases, I think it was for their own protection: soldiers actually thought, "Why would I want to put you in jeopardy?" In other cases, maybe it was to exclude them from something.

The contentious relationship between the military in the United States and the press is a hangover from the Vietnam era. The two cultures of the media and the military were able to feel each other out and realize "we're not enemies." We report bad things the military does, but we report good things as well.

If a journalist's reporting is balanced, I think most military people can live with that. It was tougher with a lot of the older soldiers who had bad memories, but I think that trust grew with time. It worked for me and the people around me. I can't say that happened in other units; I know that sometimes it didn't.

I think it's better to be close as you can be when covering a war because that's the only way you really get to see what happens. It can't be done from a remote location. It can't be done as it was in the first Gulf War, watching Norman Schwarzkopf playing little gun camera videos. Those are video games that have nothing to do with war. They're a representation of a war.

I was able to show small moments of what happens in a war. You can't be everywhere at once. You can only look in one direction at a time. Obviously, my judgment is clouded by fear. The biggest thing on my mind is "How do I stay alive?"

I didn't even notice that I was kneeling and watching a surgeon, a doctor bandaging up a soldier. Somebody mentioned it to me afterwards. That's part of the craziness of war.

Another time I was taking pictures of a prisoner being interrogated and I heard an explosion. I whipped around and didn't notice until I played it back in slow motion, but shrapnel came flying by us. I never saw it. There's a little hole in my flak jacket in the back. You really don't understand all these things that are happening even when you're there. You don't catch everything that's happening. You have to play it back in slow motion. You have to play it back in your brain in slow motion if you don't have it on tape to understand the details.

You cannot cover everything in a war. There's just too much happening. You can just take snapshots. Even if they're video, they're just small clips. Soldiers who are side-by-side see a different war. Soldiers who are hundreds of feet away from each other experience a totally different war. We never think of it that way. It always seems to be a vast landscape that the camera travels across as it does in military movies. It doesn't happen that way. It's a very small war. It's very personal.

Iraqi Civilians

Most Iraqi civilians prepared for the war. They thought it would come. They stocked up on supplies, they dug wells in their back yard for water, they had candles, they knew that there probably would be a disruption in fuel and power. The smart people actually bought live chickens to keep, because they didn't have to be refrigerated. They knew that they could kill them one at a time and have fresh meat.

When the hostility stopped, there was a sense of jubilation: Saddam was gone. I remember interviewing people the next day. One man came up to me, one man had a red, white, and blue pin that he had saved for ten years. He talked about how horrible Saddam was, how Saddam had killed his brother, had taken other family members away, and how much he loved George Bush.

It's interesting that people in places like that seem to differentiate between the United States and the citizens of the United States. In this case, early on after the war, they were very happy that Saddam was gone, and thanked the United States government. When I went back to Iraq, there were a lot of people who weren't too happy with the United States government, but who didn't blame the American citizens.

That was also in Afghanistan, where people may have disagreed with our government, but still loved the American citizens. Much of what the rest of the world sees about us as a culture is through media, is through television and films. They love all that pop culture stuff. They love McDonalds, they love Arnold Schwartzenegger, they love toys, they love computers.

People in Iraq thought that, within a week of us being there, that Iraq would be transformed into what they thought the United States was: they would have MTV and pop culture, everybody would be driving cars, people would have plenty of food, and everybody would have internet access. They actually thought that.

It was shocking to me that they thought it would transform that fast. As sad as the American preparation was for dealing with the aftermath of the war, the expectation from Iraqis about what would happen was also as unrealistic.

The American Press and Perceptions at Home

I've always said that in a combat situation, a military-type situation, that I end up burying a piece of myself there. In this war, I buried by far the biggest piece—a bigger piece than I'm ever willing to do again.

It just takes a toll, it takes a toll on you mentally, it takes a toll on you physically. I'm 40 pounds heavier than I was when I came back from Iraq. I was pretty used up, I was pretty burned out mentally, physically. I'd had malaria, I had pneumonia.

Your ability to function at that point and be sharp mentally is tough. The physical part heals. The mental part takes a lot more time. And I think it's a wound that probably never does heal in people. And it's not just for press, it's not just for military; it's for the innocent citizens.

Americans, I think, are a little softer—we don't see harsh realities of life so much. In places like Africa, people are more used to this—if it's possible to say that—in places where they see more brutality, people are more used to this. In America, we're such a litigious society. We never take responsibility for our own actions, it's gotta be somebody else's fault. If there's a problem, I'll call a lawyer! They'll figure it out. Well, it's real when it's life and death.

Lawyers don't help anything. You're responsible for your own decisions. They have a major effect on everyone around you and a lot of people make decisions that cause pain, lots of pain in your friends, in your enemy, and in innocent people. It's very, very hard, I think, to convey what war is like without being there. I think people try very hard. In the war in Iraq, this time, I think that people thought that being with the American military they would see war up close. And in many cases, they didn't. I was very dismayed by that.

The first time I had combat footage to feed back over a satellite, people on the other end were like, "Whoa, we haven't seen anything like this." That was the worse thing I heard in the whole war, besides, of course, seeing and experiencing death around me. That was just so sad to me, that so much work, so much effort would go into covering a war, and yet people never really had a sense of it. It's difficult to cover a war—it was a "live coverage of the war right now," so if it wasn't live, it was late. So people didn't make efforts to tape as much, maybe.

Some people for their own reasons chose not to put themselves in harm's way. And I'm non-judgmental about that—I would never ask anybody to do anything like that. And there were military people who for their own reasons—most of them being protective—didn't allow a journalist to be in a situation where they would be in harm's way. So we never really got to see close up what happened.

It's interesting that Al-Jazeera and the Arab-speaking news media was out-of-hand rejected in this country. And the propaganda parts of it I understand entirely, but they were able to come back with pictures from the Iraqi side that we couldn't get. And it's only because we didn't want to be in that position, I think.

I certainly did not want to be in a position where American bombs were falling on me, American shells were coming at me—I'm not that brave. I don't think I have the guts to do something like that. Maybe I had more brains, I don't know. I think it's like suicide, but—so we never saw the effect of the bombs landing, close up. Of being on the receiving end of America's military might, close up.

And I think some of the Arab services, news services, were able to capture that, although it was probably twisted a lot through propaganda purposes. The actual pictures I think we should have paid a little more attention to instead of rejecting them out of hand.

I can't say this through experience that much because I was there and I haven't seen that much what the propaganda part of the war was all about. But I do know that some of those pictures were real. And I've seen pictures of the opposite side of from where I was, and it's pretty devastating.

It puts a human face on war, and so often we don't get that. I think people try, I think news networks tried to have people covering the war from whatever angles they could, but they did not commit people to being embedded on the Iraqi side. I don't know who would be brave enough to do that.

Well, the American networks I don't think rejected out of hand showing footage that I had. There was some reticence about showing the close-up effects of war, to showing the dead bodies, the mutilated bodies, the pieces of bodies. Ultimately they showed dead bodies, but they never showed mutilated bodies or pieces of bodies.

There's a mindset that the American public needs to be spared from seeing the brutality of war close up at the dinner table, at the breakfast table. It's interesting that many of our news shows air while people are having breakfast or having dinner.

I don't share that, personally. I think that we need to show in graphic detail what war is about, and we tend not to. It's interesting that television doesn't show it, but magazines do. Things that I probably would not be able to get on network television are shown routinely in *Newsweek* or *Time*.

And I think that people can handle that. I think that Americans need to know in graphic detail about war. Decisions are made, certainly, every time they go to the voting booth. Buttons are pushed by people. They should know what it is that they're getting into, whether they're supporting a war, or not supporting a war. People need to know. Few people will ever really know, and maybe it's better that people don't. I'm not sure.

The American public really never knew that it was touch-and-go for about three days during that war. It just didn't come out. It took me three days to get those pictures back to the United States, and they were played wall-to-wall—I did a lot of television with it, and it's ironic.

I was in a vehicle, and I had a system with me that could play back live pictures while we were moving across the desert. But the very bridge that I was underneath, that was saving my life, was stopping me from transmitting those pictures back. In a live war, it's ironic that it was a piece of tape that would show the best representation of what war was.

Prior to 9/11, the coverage of foreign news was almost nonexistent in major media in the United States, and little attention was being paid by major media to what was happening in the rest of the world.

I don't know that American media is necessarily to blame for it. Times have changed. It used to be that the media would decide what was shown on media and what wasn't. Today, it's ratings-driven. If people don't watch, they don't see it. So people started to turn off foreign stories. The People Meter is a ratings system that measures what people watch on literally a moment-by-moment basis during a news show. They can tell who's watching and who's not.

And when people turn off the People Meter, they aren't shown that sort of thing as much. They're shown what they want to see, and prior to 9/11 people didn't want to see too much foreign news. One of the only silver linings to 9/11 is that Americans have become more aware of the world, it's much more complicated than they thought, that more danger is out there, that people are killing each other in a lot more places now. We're a little more aware of that right now.

What bothered me very much right after the current Gulf War, within a few weeks, was that the coverage of the war had less and less air time. Immediately, America was consumed by another story. It shocked me. Most American media shifted to cover the Laci Peterson murder story. And I didn't really understand that until I came back here and someone approached me and said, you don't know what it's like to be back here, which is true.

The center of my world was Iraq. To people here, they were watching coverage of Iraq 24-7. They watched it until they couldn't anymore, and they just had to turn away. They watched the next thing shown to them. It's not something anybody could take on a steady 24-7 basis for very long. It is horrifying. Disturbing. People don't want to watch that.

I don't think the American public understands what's happening in places like the Sudan, or Sierra Leone, or even Israel, which gets more coverage. News there tends to be reported in statistics. Five soldiers were killed. A bomb went off. It's numbers. The human side of it doesn't make it that much.

It may be a minute and 30 seconds on *NBC's Nightly News* for example. And if it's on, that's good, but it comes and it goes, it comes by like a freight train. People cannot take it on a long-term basis. It's too disturbing.

American Soldiers in Iraq

American soldiers are very highly trained, very motivated, highly equipped to wage war. By war, they mean destroying an enemy, identifying and destroying an enemy, and they do that very, very well.

Once it becomes a little murkier, once the "end of hostilities" happened, on April 9th, I remember, the light coming up. We were under a bridge, this is at objective Moe, I think, at this point—no, I'm sorry, objective Larry—I woke up the morning of April 9th, underneath a bridge called Larry, Objective Larry. And for two days, actually for three days, soldiers had been shooting at anything that came at them. And we had car bombs coming at us, RPGs, soldiers with, uh, or anybody with automatic rifles and American soldiers sat there and were destroying everything in sight.

American soldiers did very well with urban combat, urban assault. But they weren't trained very well for what was called urban patrol, or policing. On the morning of April 9th, I remember ordinary citizens coming out of houses and getting closer to where the American soldiers were, and up until then, Americans were destroying everything that was coming at them, but now they had unarmed citizens, and they didn't know how to deal with it.

I remember waking up and shouting across the intersection to a bunch of soldiers: "Welcome to Israel! You now are at a checkpoint in Israel. You get to figure out what's coming at you, are they friend or foe? Somebody's gonna put a flower in your hat or they're gonna blow you up. And you have to figure that out. Who knows any Arabic?"

Nobody knew any Arabic. "Do you have any signs in Arabic to stop people from coming at you because you're shooting at every vehicle that comes at you?"

They didn't have any signs. "Do you have any spray paint?"

Finally a soldier came up with some spray paint and put a sign up which was basically a stop sign, which people can understand around the world to stop people. And those soldiers had to figure out how to deal with the public that they couldn't distinguish from soldiers fighting against them.

By the way, the Americans, from the time they got into Baghdad had very few people with uniforms firing at them. There were people who looked like average citizens. How do you distinguish between a combatant and a non-combatant? It's very, very difficult. And as soon as the hostilities stopped, they still had to make that same decision.

I remember asking the colonel who I was with, "What now?" He looked at me and said, "Well, we were supposed to take Baghdad, we took Baghdad." "Well, but what now?" "Well, there'll be MPs, there'll be all sorts of people coming . . . " "When?" "I don't know." I asked the citizens, the few who could speak English, "What now?" It was the press, the American press—me really, that was it, I was the only person there—the American army and the Iraqi citizens just looking at us on April 9th after the shooting had stopped saying "What now?" and nobody knew. Nobody knew what to do.

There were very few translators. We had one in the battalion. By the time the shooting stopped in Baghdad, within a week or two afterwards, that person was removed to go interrogate prisoners someplace else. So here I was with 900 soldiers who were in charge of patrolling Baghdad, and nobody spoke Arabic.

On the morning of April 9th after the war ended, I remember teaching soldiers a few words in Arabic, just to try to get them to be able to deal with people. I didn't want to see people being hurt, and I thought a few words might make the difference between life or death for people. I think you have an obligation to humanity to maybe step in and try to stop someone from being killed for a mistake.

I think some soldiers were given a little card before that had a few phrases, words, but they didn't carry that into battle. Most of 'em didn't carry a wallet into battle—they never thought about things like that. How do you communicate with people? They had no way.

The Re-entry

The soldiers who went to Iraq had attitudes about the war that represented a cross-section of American attitudes about the war. Some were privately against the war: you couldn't be against it publicly. Some were really gung-ho, and some had a more complex view.

Most had a non-judgmental, practical attitude: they had a job to do. Professional soldiers who were well-trained could not let complex ideas of war get into their brain, because in combat you're trained to neutralize the enemy. You can't think about why.

Fewer people than I thought would be were gung-ho. They're

not stupid, but like the rest of Americans, the military includes a cross-section of education levels. Some soldiers are well-educated and some are less so.

I had to leave the Third Infantry Division in May 2003. They stayed there until September 2003. They were told on two occasions before then that they would leave. So there was an expectation they would leave, and that was dashed when they were told that they were gonna stay.

Then they were told they were going home again, and then they were told they were going to stay. They felt betrayed by their government in many ways. They had no relief and were very tired of being there. Most of them had been there for almost a year, some for more than a year.

It's interesting, in warfare, how things have changed over the years. In World War I or World War II, the average soldier was probably stationed for 500 days or more, and probably saw 45 days or so where they were in jeopardy. With the advent of helicopters and other changes to warfare after Korea, by Vietnam, they were seeing 250 days in jeopardy.

By the time we get to Iraq this time, the soldiers there face being in jeopardy every day, sometimes for hundreds of days in a row. That fear plays a long-term psychological game with you.

Coming back, I know soldiers found the re-entry phase difficult. I met a soldier who lives a mile and a half from my house. I never knew him. He went to the local school. His mother knows my mother. I met him in the middle of Baghdad. And I remember when he came back, I was invited to his welcome home party.

I asked him: "How is it coming back?" And he said, "Oh, it's OK." And I said, "Nah, you can tell me, how is it coming back?" His girlfriend was there, and she appeared to disapprove of my question. And I said, "You're not sleeping, you're having nightmares. You're having some anger-management problems, and that anger is sort of a free-based thing. You don't know why it is. You scare yourself."

A lot of it is being intolerant of the frivolous things in our society. It's no longer a very simple life and death, distilled life that you're living anymore, there's a lot of garbage that goes on. That bothered him, too. And I noticed he would always be looking for a weapon.

In Iraq, the people who were fighting against him didn't wear uniforms, so every civilian around him in the United States, and there, was a threat. Even though he knew all these people at this party, it still deep-seatedly bothered him. Any one of them could shoot at him. He didn't have his flak vest on. There was no one around him wearing camouflage. His buddies weren't there to protect him.

I watched him. To go to his garage, he peeked around the corner, and then looked. To go from the kitchen to the dining room, I saw him reflexively check both ways before he went through. He didn't know he was doing those things. But they're real. That's what you do. You're trained to do it. I think it wanes with time, you come down from that, but it has its effects.

*Iraqi poet **Ali Habash** was born in Baghdad in 1965 and started publishing his works in 1985. His poems have appeared in Iraqi and Arab newspapers. His first book of poetry* Years without Reason *was issued in 2001 in Tunis. His poetry has been translated into French. He is a journalist for* Al Khaleej *newspaper in the United Arab Emirates.*

Rockets Destroying a Happy Family

Ali Habash

Rockets fill my heart and head
Time is running by
All your friends are being blamed
for this, oh Iraq.
These are our dreams
Barbed wire crowds the streets
and people are entangled by it
and get lost in between.

I tried to slip through all this chaos.
I saw a family trying to climb a truck
and I saw a child with eyes
full of tears behind a tank
and I saw a coffin waiting
beside the Euphrates bank.

Life has no meaning anymore.
Just tons of metal and iron
Are all these arms just for me,
For my children, my old home?

Sinan Antoon was born in Iraq in 1967, Sinan Antoon is a poet, novelist, and filmmaker. He studied English literature at Baghdad University before coming to the United States after the 1991 Gulf War. He currently teaches Arabic and Arabic literature at Dartmouth College. This narrative is excerpted from his interview with Rick King for the film Voices in Wartime.

Everything That Was Beautiful Is Gone

Sinan Antoon

My own childhood was defined by war. I was 12 when I witnessed the first war, and since then it's been non-stop. When you are also plagued with being a political being, and you follow the news and read every day, you know that wars are being waged all over the place. You can't escape it.

When I was growing up, I saw men being sentenced to death for no reason. People who I grew up with—people who I played soccer with—had to be drafted and were taken away when they were eighteen because they didn't go to college.

I remember one of my closest friends was depressed because he didn't want to go. Every 23 days they would have a six-day break, and at the end of his break he would be suffering and crying because he didn't want to go back to the battlefront. But if you didn't go back, you got executed.

I had to deal with these things very early on. It's terrible, but seeing death and suffering, you get to appreciate life and you get to appreciate these brief moments that we have with beauty, with love, with peace. Unfortunately all of these things work in a Manichaean way. You never really appreciate peace unless you see, or you try to know what war is all about. I guess it's made me a more tender person. War makes you more human somehow.

In the 1980s, when I grew up, you would ask someone how they were doing and a kid of six or seven years old would tell you "I'm depressed." Depression entered the discourse of the young people. Even if you didn't go into combat and fight yourself, you saw people around you—your neighbors, your relatives—dying. You knew that everyone's existence was fragile and that they could die. You saw men you grew up with coming back in coffins.

There were no dreams. Everything was shattered. People's expectations were so low. Many of my friends or relatives spent the years from age 18 until 37, the best years of their lives, fighting a war they did not believe in at a time when the enlightened West was supporting that war. Saddam was the sweetheart.

But the tragedy comes with the sanctions after both the Iran-Iraq War and the 1990 war, which completely destroyed the infrastructure. Whatever we feel or say about Saddam, we feel or say rightly so; he's a vicious dictator. But there was a functioning country, there was infrastructure. The 1990-91 war destroyed the infrastructure and the sanctions ensured that that infrastructure would never be rebuilt.

Saddam invaded Kuwait and the so-called international community—the civilized world—wanted to force him to leave Kuwait, so they imposed sanctions on him. But the sanctions didn't work, so we went to war. He was ejected out of Kuwait, but the sanctions were maintained, supposedly because the sanctions would weaken the regime.

Now we know that these were the most devastating sanctions in history ever. Everything was considered dual-use that could potentially be used for weapons of mass destruction: Pencils for school kids because of the lead inside them, all kinds of medicines, antibiotics. You had the systematic destruction of a whole society, especially the middle class, especially the intelligentsia. A professor's salary would not be enough to buy an egg, for example. You had the complete crumbling of the economy. You had people selling their furniture, people selling their doors. People were leaving en masse. Four and a half million Iraqis left during the 1990s.

The Human Cost

I was watching the war while in Cairo. I was living in Egypt at the time. I watched the war on a daily basis because I could. I was glued to the TV and watching the aftermath of the war. When I was in Iraq and people—Iraqis abroad or others—would say it was difficult to see other human beings you care about going through war and not be there.

Sometimes it's even more difficult not being there. I was watching the complete destruction that war brings always, but also all of the mass graves that were exhumed. These mass graves were the result of the 1991 war, when President Bush—the father—called on Iraqis to stage an uprising, to take things into their own hands. They did stage an uprising, but they were not supported.

Not only were they not supported, but Saddam was also allowed by the ceasefire signed with Norman Schwarzkopf to use helicopters to slaughter all of these people. Later, Schwarzkopf in his memoirs said "Well I didn't know that. He said that he was going use them to transfer the wounded. I didn't know that he was going to use them in unspeakable—" There is a certain complicity. But I was watching the mass graves and watching the mothers crying over their children, who are civilians, and not soldiers, who are people who are not pro-Saddam. It is the people caught in the war.

The human loss that comes with war was the impetus behind that poem. There was one scene in particular of an actual man in a city in southern Iraq who had lost nine members of his family. He was standing, and there were nine coffins there. The picture was in *The New York Times* and other places. He was just saying that he didn't know which one to mourn first. The weight of this suffering started a cycle of images, and that's how the poem was born.

I left in 1991 because I was an artist, a poet. I was suffocating. I always wanted to leave. The sad thing is that in returning last July after 13 years, I observed that it's still a decrepit place. You see the destruction of people's lives, their psyches. You see the wrinkles on their faces and that people have aged so much more in 13 years. You hear the sighs when people talk.

Even those few places in Baghdad that I used to run to because they were still beautiful and not marred by Saddam's images or murals are completely barren now. There is so much trash, so much garbage—all of this chaos because of the war.

It's really terrible and this is the feeling that most Iraqis or all

Iraqis who go back feel. Yes, it was terrible to live under Saddam but even those tiny places or spaces that had remained beautiful are now completely destroyed.

A few weeks before this last war, an Iraqi artist—a woman who was in the opposition against Saddam and forced to leave Iraq—wrote something very poignant. She said that if this war started, the Iraq that so many of us knew would be gone forever. It's true, in a way.

I always had this instinctive feeling, even when I was ten, that something was amiss. I knew that Saddam was bad before realizing history and politics. I had no qualms about leaving Iraq. I abhor nationalism. I'm not a nationalist.

I thought I'd prepared myself because I followed the news every day and I was active about the sanctions and the war. During the war, I couldn't do any work; I just watched the satellite channels. The Arab satellite channels had more presence there. I thought that I'd already seen the extent of the damage.

But going there was really, really terrible—not just because the people that I knew are now completely drained and old, with wrinkles on their faces, but also because of the cracks in the houses. Everything that was beautiful is completely gone now. Even the palm trees—my last refuge—looked really dry and sick.

It wasn't a great city, but when I was there in July there was complete chaos. There was garbage all over the place, uncollected garbage. And there were barbed wires. The whole urban space is really ugly now because you have this new class of war merchants who are the product of the 1990s. There were all these commodities all over on the sidewalks.

I'm not complaining. I know we need commodities, but I searched for the places that I'd liked, and they were not there, or they were completely obliterated. The place was dead, as far as I'm concerned. It's different for the people who are living there. Again, I have this luxury of saying the place is dead for me and it's over. But there are people there who have to live with this reality. It was very sad.

Despite everything, I was heartened that there are artists; there are people working to start a civil society—young people, men and women, starting organizations under very difficult circumstances. What I heard most from everyone was "We are tired. We are drained. We can't take this anymore."

There is this bitterness towards people who left. I went somewhere to film a place and some man told me, "You look like you're one of those who are coming back from abroad." I was kind of hurt.

I told him, "I am not here to do business and steal your money. I'm not here to rule you. I'm not into opposition. I'm here to make a documentary about your suffering. So give me some respect."

He switched to the other extreme, and I just reasoned with him. I asked him "Had you had the opportunity to leave in 1991, wouldn't you have left?" And he said "Yes."

There is a bitterness with the Iraqis inside, especially towards the people the U.S. is choosing to govern them, most of whom have spent 30 years abroad. So a lot of people told me, "We want someone who's lived with us under these conditions, who understands what we've gone through. We don't want someone who's lived 35 years abroad in five-star hotels to come now and tell us how we should live our life."

Unfortunately, most of the candidates who are promoted by this administration are these people who've been abroad for 35 years and who are, in a way, professional opposition people. They're businessmen. They're not activists. They don't have a constituency inside. It's sadly very reminiscent of exactly what the British did when they occupied Iraq.

It's amazing how some of the same patterns repeat themselves. The amazing thing is that the General who led the British troops in invading Iraq, said "We don't come as conquerors; we come as liberators." In a moment of, perhaps, colonialism speaking through people, Rumsfeld said the same exact words. He said "We are not conquerors, we are liberators." Most Iraqis don't see the Americans as liberators. It's important for Americans to know that the world does not perceive us as liberators.

Poetry's Impact

You feel—we feel—what can poetry do? The reactions that I get from people reading poetry is that it expresses what they feel. It means something to them. When I went back, I was invited to read at the Union of Iraqi Writers. I recited my poetry, and there was a certain apprehension on my part because I had been away and all of that.

The reaction of the people there, the young writers, was very sweet. They really welcomed me in, and they were happy that someone who had been away for so long was still in contact and was still writing things that could express how they feel.

During the difficult times leading to the war and the first few months of the war, the things that I wrote in Arabic and English generated lot of e-mails from Iraqis and others—even Americans—that said that it helped them go through that phase. I don't want to self-aggrandize, but that's the highest accolade for me.

Primarily, you write for yourself, but you're living in a world, and you know that the cultural products get consumed and circulated. When I went through some really difficult times, and when I was in the darkness of the shelter under the bombing, hearing that other people abroad—people I didn't know—were demonstrating for me, were screaming, were writing poetry and articles, made a difference.

It's like the difference between dying alone or dying knowing that someone is mourning you or sympathizing with you. It makes a great difference. It could be, a romantic, old-fashioned feeling, but I still believe in our species. It's a responsibility I feel, personally. If one is able to express something, then they should do that, and they should share it with others.

In Arab culture, poetry occupies a unique position because of the heritage of the oral poetry that was revered and the function of the poet in pre-Islamic times. It was mainly an oral culture, and for some reason poetry was very developed already by the seventh century.

Poetry was the register—the archive—of life. Especially with the Bedouin nomadic life, it was, like all other cultural production, a way through which people made sense of their lives. But then with the advent of Islam and *The Koran* being claimed by Mohammed to be the word of God, there was this kind of approach to language as sacred. There was a kind of symbiosis between the pre-Islamic poetry and *The Koran* itself. It was used to explain it.

For many reasons, we had an amazing number of great poets.

Poetry continued—and continues to this day—to be the most valued art form. The novel has made encroachments and advances, but poetry still is very revered by Arabs.

There's always talk of the crisis that poetry faces worldwide, but in the Arab world it's still different. For example, the Palestinian poet Mahmud Darwish can fill a stadium when he recites poetry. Forty-thousand people show up. People still do read and listen, and poems are events. Poetry really matters, especially during the war. People resort to poetry to go through difficult times.

Even Saddam himself knew the importance of this, and there was a complete militarization of culture as well. He made sure to pump a lot of money into trying to tame and domesticate all the poets. Those who were not willing to write panegyrics or who were against the regime were executed. Some of them were put in prison. Some of them had to leave the country and have been living in exile for 35 years. Poetry is a very potent thing in the Arab world, and especially in Iraq because of the history it has.

When I started writing and I took some of the poems to publish in the journals, I was told that they were very beautiful, and that I was talented, but that they were too sad. For example, if a poem featured a man who dies in the war and has a mother who wears black, I was told to change that because His Excellency the President says that a mother should be happy and proud that her son had died.

There were certain written and unwritten rules about what to write, and everyone had to write and to celebrate the regime, celebrate the war. If you didn't write that kind of poetry, there was no place for you. You were completely marginalized.

I personally chose not to publish inside. I only published abroad when I was there. In 1989, I sent a poem to a journal in Paris, and it was published there. But the local journals would never publish my stuff. They basically told me, "This is too depressing, and we are not going to publish this." But I'm proud that I did that because there aren't many.

Now, after the fall of the regime, there is this openness with newspapers in the cultural circles. There is an accounting for those who sold their souls to the regime, the poets, the writers, and the people who were responsible. At least I can say that I never wrote one word in praise of the regime.

War After War

Right after the end of the Iran-Iraq War in 1988, there was a big celebration. Most of the people just felt happy that they were going to go back to their normal lives and peace. People were joking that it was going to be at least another five years before Saddam got us into another war.

But just 17 months after that, it became obvious that there was going to be another war. It saddens me thinking of these young children whose lives would forever be marred by war, or thinking of all the mothers, wives, and sisters who were happy that their men were going to come back. Then it was all shattered because they all had to go back to war to their deaths.

That was the impetus behind the poem "A Prism: Wet with Wars," and the whole feeling of suffocation. When you open a window, you want to look out on something else, something more hopeful. But you feel you are besieged by wars, and that wherever you go there is just another war.

Sadly—not that it is prophetic, but it happened again in 1991 and 2003—that is how I think a lot of the Iraqis feel. Most of their lives they've lived under the threat of wars, either an impending war or an actual war. That's the story behind the poem.

I try sometimes to write about other things, but it's always like a tiny window that gets shut really quickly. People have told me—friends or people who read my material regularly—that there is more blood, more bones, and [that] it's all very bleak.

But we live in a very bleak world, so that's how it affects me personally. You can't escape it in a way. It's very bloody, and the bloodiness is showing in the writing and in the tone, a very sad tone. Throughout history, poetry and culture . . . help us make sense of this world and make reality tolerable.

Reality, in a way, is intolerable. But cultural production—poetry, music, film—it's like this prism that enables us to see the world, and go through it, and survive.

The Exile of Language

The linguistic exile is the most difficult thing, although my English is really good because I studied English literature. My mom was American, so I heard some English at home. My father was Iraqi, and my mother was American.

As a poet, a linguistic being, you savor the language. You hear it, you read it, you see it, and then you lose all of that. It's very difficult. You feel cut off from the pace of life. Having to work there, there is no time to read and keep up. For a long time I was afraid that I had lost touch. Also, I wasn't able to write for a very long time.

Thank God for the Internet. There are all these amazing web sites where many people who write poetry in Arabic—men and women—are bypassing the cultural mafias and the editors [with] their own web sites. I can go to a web site and read the poems written by a woman in Morocco, or someone in Egypt, or exchange an e-mail. The Internet has bridged the gap.

People like Edward Said have written that exile as well gives you a certain privilege, a certain perspective. I didn't have to go through the sanctions, like others did. And I have a certain space and a luxury of having the time to read, ponder, or complain that I don't write poetry that others don't.

This is the irony, I guess, of history: that all of the suffering produces beautiful culture. Thanks to Saddam and to Bush—the father, we have a burgeoning Diaspora of literature because four and one-half million Iraqis left the country. The poets and writers and artists are all over the world— in Sweden, in Australia, in New Zealand, here.

It's amazing you read the papers and see the books and see Iraqi writers living in Sweden or Moscow. After awhile, they interact with the local cultures; they see different languages. I'm privileged and lucky because I get to pursue my literary studies. I get to interact with the culture here. I read in other languages. I can't complain.

After awhile, exile becomes home, and home is not home anymore. You feel at home not being at home. I knew that was going to happen, from having this penchant for reading about people who are in exile. I knew that when I returned to Iraq after 13 years, whatever had been Iraq for me would not exist anymore. You get used to being away, being cut off.

Life Under Occupation

I got a letter from my childhood friend, my neighbor. I grew up with her. I asked her in my e-mail how life was: She said "I'm crying now as I'm writing this to you because I don't know if we're going to live to the next day."

She's a working woman and she has to go across town to go to work. She sees all these suicide cars and suicide bombs. She talks about the humiliation, the daily humiliation she has to go through, because of all these checkpoints . . . the barbed wire.

Life is intolerable for most people, especially the middle class, and especially women and children. Women bore the brunt of the suffering during the sanctions. We live in a patriarchal world, but in societies that are even more patriarchal, women—the vulnerable— are the ones who pay the higher price.

There were high rates of suicide amongst women during the sanctions in the 1990s because they could not support their families. Now, working women cannot go to work for safety concerns. When I was there in July, many girls were not going to school because they were being raped and kidnapped. Only those girls whose parents could accompany them to school were going. Imagine what this is going to do to education.

It's telling that when Rumsfeld was asked about the chaos—the chaos that could have been avoided—he said, "This is what happens, like after the Bulls win the NBA." This is the level with which this guy looks.

According to international law, when you occupy a country, you're responsible for the security. It's not such a great feat. It was very simple. Why didn't they impose a curfew the first day of occupation? A curfew would have solved a lot of problems. But there was no curfew imposed. I'm still trying to find answers and to grapple with that.

It's very sad that we have to say that it's a lousy occupation. It's very lousy because it's intertwined with local politics here. The administration sends all these young, young kids, who have no knowledge of the Middle East, to Iraq as kickbacks. We know the companies that are getting all the contracts. It's very sad.

With the way the British troops are dealing in Southern Iraq, there have been far, far fewer incidents in terms of disturbances and problems. The British deal with the population in a respectful way. The irony of this situation is that it's because the British have this colonial memory; they have experience.

Having a gripe with occupation doesn't mean that you loved Saddam and you want him back. Everyone should stay away from this dichotomy. But the reality is what do people all over the world want? They want a simple life, security, and safety. Okay. Saddam is gone, and there was euphoria. But, as I said, under Saddam there were parameters. If you said something against the regime, if you expressed dissatisfaction, you would suffer. You would go in.

But at least you knew what the parameters were. If you do not chastise the regime, if you do not say something terrible about Saddam, if you do your job, you stay away, you live. At least you could secure that.

Now it's complete chaos. The social contract is completely gone. You cannot guarantee anything. You could be walking down the street and you would be killed for no reason. People have a right to say that it was better under Saddam—not for everyone. I saw graffiti when I was in Baghdad on the walls saying, "If democracy means theft, crime, and rape, then we don't want this democracy."

Because of the chaos even in the values and in the moral system, people who have new cars don't take their cars out. Criminals, after the long years of sanctions, have become so efficient that if you don't vacate your car within ten seconds, you're shot in the head right away.

I met a woman who is carrying a gun now because she's a doctor, and she has to go to her clinic. Now she is carrying a gun because if she's attacked, she's going to kill people. Imagine the level of militarization.

Because there is no police, and because when the U.S. came in they immediately disbanded the army and the police, there was this void. People were talking about a lot of bodies lying around in the outskirts of Baghdad because these thugs were killing people and leaving them out there. Not only are there no police, but there is no functioning health care system.

Wrinkles on the Wind's Forehead

Sinan Antoon

1

the wind is a blind mother
stumbling
over the corpses
no shrouds
save the clouds
but the dogs
are much faster

2

the moon is a graveyard
for light
the stars women
wailing

3

the wind was tired
from carrying the coffins
and leaned
against a palm tree
A satellite inquired:
Where to now?
the silence
in the wind's cane murmured:
"Baghdad"
and the palm tree caught fire

4

the soldier's fingers scrape
and scrabble

like question marks
or sickles
they search the womb
of the wind
for weapons
. . .
nothing but smoke
and depleted uranium

5

how narrow is this strait
which sleeps
between two wars
but I must cross it

6

My heart is a stork
perched on a distant dome
in Baghdad
its nest made of bones
its sky
of death

7

This is not the first time
myths wash their face
with our blood
(t)here they are
looking in horizon's mirror
as they don our bones

8

war salivates
tyrants and historians pant
a wrinkle smiles
on the face of a child
who will play
during a break
between wars

9

The Euphrates
is a long procession
Cities pat its shoulders
as palm trees weep

10

The child plays
in time's garden
but war calls upon her
from inside:
come on in!

11

The grave is a mirror
into which the child looks
and dreams:
when will I grow up
and be like my father:
dead

12

the Tigris and Euphrates
are two strings
in death's lute
and we are songs
or fingers strumming

13

For two and a half wars
I've been here
in this room
whose window is a grave
that I'm afraid of opening
there is a mirror on the wall
when I stand before it
naked
my bones laugh
and I hear death's fingers
tickling the door

14

I place my ear
on the belly of this moment
I hear wailing
I put it on another moment
— the same!

Growing Up in the Shadow of Guns

/

Chris Abani

Chris Abani *is a Nigerian war survivor, human rights activist and refugee, author of three poetry collections and two novels, recipient of the 2001 PEN U.S.A. Freedom-to-Write Award, the 2001 Prince Claus Award, and a 2003 Lannan Literary Fellowship. This narrative is excerpted from his interview with Rick King for the film* Voices in Wartime.

~

I was born just as the Nigerian-Biafran War was starting in 1966. For much of the war, I was a toddler. My particular family made our way out as refugees and much of that narrative of what happened during that war was received from parents, and from elder brothers.

My eldest brother was actually detained and they were going to turn him into a boy soldier. He was nine or ten. I am actually bigger than him physically and he talks about lugging me on his back for miles and miles and miles.

We came back to Nigeria when I was five. This was about 1970, 1971. After the so-called peace and the "No Victors No Vanquished" treaty, the federal government instituted cantonments of soldiers all across the Igbo hinterlands to make sure that there would be no recurrence of this rebellion.

And so all of us grew up with the shadow of soldiers around us, with guns. There would be road blocks. You would be in the car coming home from school with your father or mother and they would be humiliated. It's like if you watch what's happening in the West Bank now. Israel is humiliating the Palestinians. It's not even about security anymore. It's about eradicating a human being's right to any kind of dignity as a kind of way to quell any kind of rebellion against you.

And the war stayed around. I remember one particular time,

the army, the guy who ran the particular cantonment near the house
I grew up in, lived about five miles away. He had this beautiful house
on a hill. And he was known for picking young girls up on the streets
and raping them and this kind of stuff. So finally, some people set
fire to his house one day. And I remember coming home from school
to watch this blaze, and with a whole group of people who were
laughing. This was their only sort of revenge.

And so it builds into your psyche in that way. From the first
coup in 1966 right up to even now with what we call pretend
democracy in Nigeria, the military have overshadowed every form of
government and politics. The gun has been the way which we are
run. So we have become a brutalized people.

And of course no one has ever dealt with the trauma of the war.
The Igbos just wanted to put it behind them and get ahead. But all
the time it begins to surface and surface and people who are born
who are just 16 years old talk about waging another war.

It's kind of frightening how much this has been internalized. I
grew up playing in burnt-out tanks, in front of my primary school,
picking up bullets that were still live, playing football, and running
into hamlets that still had skulls in them and things like this. As a
child you don't realize until you're an adult and can contemplate this
in a way, how much this impacts your thinking.

I think there's a lot of callousness and brutality in Nigeria in
general, which is a result of that war and that has never been
talked about. And the real problem right now is that you can see
the portents of another war coming.

The Legacy of Colonialism

Nigeria is about four times the size of the United Kingdom. It's a
huge country. It's a very populous country we're talking about,
around 150 million to 200 million people. But it's a Nigeria that
doesn't really exist. It's a phantom.

In the late 19th century when the Western powers coalesced the
colonial experience, Africa was divided up into countries. Whole
nations and ethnic groups were cut up into a shape to suit whatever
territories were being negotiated in this way. So what you have is
250, possibly 300, ethnic groups jammed together in one landmass

who've never had to live together as a nation before, with about the same number of languages: 250 languages, 2000 dialects. Also distinct levels of religious practice, as well as the various levels of animism through Islam and the Catholic Church and whatever is jammed together in this entity called Nigeria.

Nigeria's only 30, maybe 40 years old. It's a country that is wealthy, that produces so much oil; that has gold, uranium, and diamonds. But it is not located equally across the country. When already the issue of ethnicity is so much on the razor's edge, you then add economic conditions so that some groups seem to be better off than others, you really create a melting pot for trouble.

The conflict, the particular war, which I suppose has been the model for wars in Africa, (and that's not a good thing to say), was the Nigerian-Biafran War. Its roots are way back in pre-independence.

We got independence in 1960. The country was divided up. The politicians were in power. And soon enough, the issues of ethnicity and who controls what begins to create a lot of trouble. So around 1963, 1964, the assembly, the house of the senate, people are pulling guns on each other in the house of the senate. These are politicians.

So the military steps in and declares a state of emergency and attempts to sort of contain things to allow democracy to find its feet. Well, when the military pulls out, the problem continues. So a group of young officers in the army, primarily southerners—Igbos and a few from the central part of Nigeria—organize a coup against the incumbent government. And in the process of the coup (coups are never bloodless), a lot of Northern politicians were murdered.

A military government was set up to create the peace, which was then run by an Igbo, an adjutant, he's supposedly a young Northerner, Yakubu Gowon. And six months after this coup, there was pressure from Northerners, of which Yakubu Gowon was one, to retaliate, which was considered an Igbo-incited coup. There was a coup against the military government and this head of state was murdered by his own adjutant over dinner in front of his children.

That's the story. I don't know if this is urban legend or actually what happened, but then the country begins to experience this problem where in the North, under the guise of religion, the Igbos are targeted in a program of ethnic cleansing. In six months, over

200,000 Igbos are murdered. Their bodies are cut up and their body parts are put in trains. The trainloads of dead Igbos are being sent back down to the South by Northerners.

The then-governor of the East/Central region where the Igbos lived, Lt. Col. Ojukwu, asked the government to step in and asked "Why aren't you sending soldiers to contain this?" When the government wouldn't say anything, he demanded that all Southerners return back to the Eastern region. He then seceded from the rest of Nigeria and declared us an independent republic called Biafra.

The Northerners went along with this originally. In Ghana, there was something signed called the Aburi Accord that allowed us to secede. But when they return, the Nigerians realize that all the oil is suddenly going away with the Republic of Biafra, and they declare a war against us and say you can't secede. And of course then all the power interests around the world who want the oil begin to back Nigeria.

I think that Lyndon Johnson was president at the time, and he backed Nigeria. He's alleged to have said we cannot afford to have a Japan in Africa: Biafra must be crushed. And there are reasons behind this. The Biafrans invented the things now being used in Brazil, where we have cars run on sugarcane fuel. This was invented in the Biafran War. All this sort of stuff was happening during this war period and it seemed important to crush us.

So you have the fledgling state with no guns. A lot of the people fought with clubs and machetes against a fully armed government that had troops that were trained by everyone. The only countries who supported us militarily essentially were France and a little bit from Israel.

And we had no airplanes. We had these little Piper two-seater planes, and someone would hang out the side with a machine gun. We were fighting big jets. And so the resistance was still strong and we managed.

The Biafrans pushed very close to the capitol of Lagos and would have succeeded, but over the course of time the government of Nigeria changed tactics and began to use hunger as a way to win the war. Orders were given to shoot down the Red Cross planes, which were largely funded by the Portuguese under a Catholic emergency system.

All the planes that brought in food and medical supplies were being shot down. They were killing all the missionaries who had stayed back to help. They were killing all the Red Cross officials. So essentially what happened is that the Biafrans began to starve to death.

And during that three-year war over one-million children starved to death, that have been accounted for. We can't begin to talk about the bodies that have never been found. That essentially brought the whole thing to a close: starvation tactics.

So you can sort of see the arc of how it happens. And you read about Rwanda 20 or 30 years later or even Sierra Leone happening now and it's remarkable how we never seem to learn from anything that goes on prior to us. The same tactics are being employed, which are starvation and mutilation of people.

Which is another thing. The Northern soldiers would get pregnant women and cut them open and drag out the fetuses. Everything, all the conflicts, have been manufactured as ideas of ethnicity and religion. But of course there are deeper issues at play here.

And often the silent players who are outside the continent are never seen. Who really instigates wars. The role of the CIA. But not as a way to apologize for what we've done. It doesn't matter what someone engineers, you're the one killing your own people and so there are things to be accounted for now.

On the Biafran side, it was very hard to have a civilian life. We had no army, the army was a civilian army, so civilians signed up and a lot of the people were students, university students. There were so many women who fought in this war, whose own story has not even been scratched. It's always talked about: the heroic way of men, and I think I resisted that in my portrayal of it.

Children as Decoys

Similar to Vietnam where children were used as decoys, it's very hard to separate a civilian population sometimes when you are fighting a guerrilla war.

But for those who were there, there were women who cut off parts of their body to cook and feed to their children. This is not imagined.

This is true. If you are a woman and your children are dying, there are women who killed and helped suffocate their children because there was no way they would have survived the war. These women just couldn't deal with this trauma anymore for their children. Within the war there was the hunger, the starvation, the women who had to enter into prostitution on both sides with both their supposed attackers and defenders in order to negotiate a life.

There were also men who sold each other out, people who enacted their own darkness on other people. If you look at the Second World War, where there has been a lot of writing and movies and things made about it, you see that darkness all the time. Seemingly nice, normal people will turn on their neighbors for no apparent reason if it can be justified in a larger context. These are some of the effects the Nigerian-Biafran Civil War had.

In every war there is cannibalism, and nobody talks about it. One of the most amazing things that has emerged recently is tales of the concentration camps in Germany, and of how people would eat each other and not talk about it afterwards.

For me there is no subject, if we are to regain any kind of internal moral landscape, there can be nothing that is not to be confronted. So, in the civilian population, as you were being done to and in order to survive, you begin to enact in your own small way little violences on each other. There are stories of people who would lead soldiers to where other people were hiding out and watch them be executed. There was the pretext of taking bodies away to be buried: there is no meat, you make meat.

These things happen, and in order to not have the Western population point at you as a savage, you cover these stories up. This is not right because we know stories from Vietnam where soldiers would mutilate bodies in Vietnam and wear garlands of ears. This is what war does. There is nothing pretty about it. There is nothing heroic about it. And on that level in the war, this is what happens to the civilian population.

People lost their property when they had to move out of certain parts of the country and that property was occupied by other people. People lost all their money. They would come back and try to start a new life after the war. You notice petty little hierarchies emerging where some people can deal with the invader better than others, so they begin to play off their own population.

It's not unique and what's really sad about it, is that it's not unique to any war situation. It's the same and has been the same since Julius Caesar invaded the Celts. It's the same story and it's the one story we just can't seem to learn the lesson from. We seem to do well in every other field, but in this need to enact violence on each other we just don't seem to be able to figure out what the narrative is.

The Isolation of Americans

America is a very insular country in a sense and I think a lot of what happens outside of America is unknown to Americans. I think to Americans, Africa largely remains a dark continent; a place that is just where stereotypes run rampant, in a sense. But I think the Biafran War is very present in America in the 1960s American consciousness, because this was a war being fought at the same time that the Vietnam War was being fought, and there was already a sort of sensationalism to it.

But when the consciousness moved from the 1960s to the 1970s and to very different areas, the subsequent wars that have happened have been glazed over with the beauty of people like CNN who offer you almost a video-game reportage of wars.

Even within Africa as well, the sad thing is that a country like Nigeria, which is at the forefront economically (outside of South Africa we are the richest, most populous sub-Saharan country), and with Rwanda, we would stand back and watch it happen knowing they shared a history. Thirty years after the war, people talk about it like it was last week. They will stand back and watch Sierra Leone happen.

And I know that we sent troops into it, but it was more of a PR exercise than it was anything else. I think there is always a tendency in human nature to justify our current actions with historical precedents. Rather than a war serving as a warning, the war becomes a way to justify the current war, in a way. Any sort of tenuous gains made by it are trumpeted out of proportion, and none of the real impact is discussed in any sort of way. Wars sadly serve as models for other wars to be based on. And you look at the Pentagon, where they are not looking for a way to end war, but for a way to fight a war without any loss on their side.

It's about the myth of war. In the book I talk about the journey through and how you see all this devastation until after a while you realize the war is nothing but a self-perpetuated state. After a while everyone forgets what it's about because it's about nothing but itself.

And if you went in to ask the Tutsis or the Hutus what was really the issue, nobody would be able to tell you. And that's what's really sad. It seems to me that all the darkness in our souls seems to be channeled into this one moment and we hang on to grudges and all sorts of things that don't make any sense, even mental problems are hung on this need to dispense with the other.

And so wars always require the creation of others. The Palestinian, not as person but as a bomber. The Israeli, not as an invader but as a long-suffering person. And the difficulty of course with a lot of narratives is if you have suffered any great tragedy yourself, it seems that people use that to deny their impact on a thing.

So, for instance, Israel. Because of the terrible, terrible holocaust that happened to Jewish people, the moment you call Sharon or anyone else to say "Listen, look at what you are doing," the Holocaust argument is thrown in your face as a way to prevent you from having that conversation. The Igbos in Nigeria will use the Civil War and the pogroms used against them as a shield not to discuss why there needs to be dialogue between us and the Northerners to ease tensions. Then the Hutus claim that the Tutsis had oppressed them in the past. There always seems to be a narrative of previous suffering.

I became a poet while trying to express my period as a political prisoner. That experience. Because I started off as a fiction writer, and just the intensity of that experience was better portrayed in poetry. Partly because poetry allows people to come into a really profound and gut-wrenching experience, and stepping out of it almost like frames of still photography rather than the full-length feature a novel gives.

I had always read poetry as a child. I had poetry read to me. In terms of writing, the first time I really took that on seriously was in writing "Kalakuta Republic."

What really drew me to poetry, I suppose you could say, is the brevity of it. It is a distillation, but really it has more to do with the fact that you have a smaller palette you're working with. A smaller palette, and therefore you cannot begin too many emotional directions. It's a form that resists sentimentality. And when you are dealing with a difficult subject, sentimentality is a problem because you're sign-posting how people should feel.

You want to create essentially almost religious icons that hang in a cloister and one meditates on it and brings the emotional baggage with the reader rather than providing it for them. You are providing access at so many different levels. That aspect to poetry is really beautiful.

The poem "Break a Leg" comes from two places and several photographs taken by an American photographer from *Life* magazine who was murdered, who was killed; he never came back from the Biafran War. There is a photograph he took of a young soldier, who has no leg, with an AK-47 with Jesus taped to the stalk of his gun barrel. But also I have an older relative who fought in the war who was 12 years old, a soldier, and his whole foot was torn off by a claymore mine. Here is "Break a Leg":

His foot, torn off at the ankle,
Half wrapped in corrugated iron

Held the promise of a gift.
Jesus smiled sadly from the

Photo taped to his gun's stock.
Blood, like the rain, soaked everything.

The medic, impotent,
Suspicious, like God, lied.

So it was a combination of those kind of moments where you have received a narrative. I have the visual images from books that have been written, analytical books and also family anecdotes and then people you grew up around.

I went to primary school at six or seven, with people who had been soldiers during the war.. They were 13, 14 and their school had been interrupted, but they had killed men. If you had any money you could give them a little bit of money and they would cut themselves. I saw the effects of this growing up all the time. It's a result of perception, some kind of latent genetic memory. Who knows what you see when you are two? How it layers into your emotional make-up, received narrative, and research? "Break a Leg" came from that, and several other poems in the book that enact themselves in the same way.

The Prophecies of a Poet

Christopher Okigbo died during the Biafran War. He was a poet who decided it was not enough to write or to work for the broadcasting service. So he went on to the front lines and he was murdered, essentially by betrayal.

He wrote a book a year before the war happened, in 1965. And there were poems prophesizing the war. He knew this war was coming. There's a particular poem called "Come Thunder" and you can just see this war coming. It's like reading "The Second Coming" by Yeats. It's as if the portents are always there and the portents are there now.

Chris was an intriguing character. He, Wole Soyinka, and Chinua Achebe all came out of the same arts movement in the 1960s when there were visual artists and all of that. But Chris was one of the most amazing poets ever produced, not just in his ability to reach back into traditions, the European and Yeats, but also in his ability to see into the heart of the matter.

And he believed that poetry was powerful enough to effect some kind of change or to halt some kind of progress. And I think for him, (and this is entirely my perception of it, Chris died before I was born,) I think the moment he lost faith was when the war happened anyway. In spite of all the warnings. He lost faith in the power of poetry and I think for him that's when he became a full-fledged soldier. He felt that the gun was the only answer.

For me it's kind of a conflicted thing. For me to be an artist means to be immersed in a thing but also to stand away from it. To have some kind of objective distance, to observe what is happening in the moment. And to be absorbed in the moment makes it difficult to be anything more than polemic. But also there are questions of what artists owe to the society in which they live. Chris is dead and all they have are fragments of poems that maybe fill two or three collections.

There is an interesting book by Ali Mazrui which is called *The Trial of Christopher Okigbo* where he puts him on trial in heaven. He has to defend the reason why he gave up on his art in order to take up the gun.

Wole, who is not an Igbo, publicly decries on the BBC the government's policy of starving children to death, and gets arrested and spends three years in prison in solitary confinement. Wole Soyinka was the first official political prisoner we had ever had. But, that whole generation not only believed in the power of art to change things but also felt that the artists had a responsibility to society. I think Christopher Okigbo, Wole Soyinka, and Chinua Achebe in that way sort of represent the possibility of transmutation.

There's an amazing thing that Wole Soyanka said in a book called *The Man Died*. He said every moment we are silent in the face of tyranny, that which is human in us dies a little bit. So you are either enacting it directly or by acquiescence, or it is enacted upon you and there is no way that can happen that you cannot be scarred by it.

What separates us as human from the rest of the life forms on the planet is that elusive thing that we are trying to pretend away, which is called a conscience. It doesn't matter what arguments you make for it, damaged childhood whatever, the point is there would be no need to create defenses against violence if violence were a natural state for us.

Stabat Mater

Chris Abani

Through gaps in trees, moonlight
veins night with the remembrance of

dawn. Among ferns stubbling the forest
floor a mother squats, watching the child in

her arms losing its grip on life,
its hacking breath, a suffering hanging on.

Gently she closes her eyes as her fingers
pincer its nose and mouth,

easing the passage across.
What detail can be true of the remembered life;

Place, event, lost like a flower's scent
stolen by a bee leaving only the itch of its sting

He Went Out One Day, and Never Came Back

/

Antonieta Villamil

Author of seven books, **Antonieta Villamil** *is an international award-winning bilingual poet, narrator, editor, translator and activist. Her work focuses on the forgotten ones and honors them with a voice. Villamil edits and translates the collection* Poetry Solos/Solos de Poesìa, *directs the poetry workshop and the press* Casa de Poesìa / House of Poetry, *the poetry review* Moradalsur *and a Spanish language radio show for KPFK 90.7 FM Los Angeles, on contemporary poets. This narrative is excerpted from Antonieta Villamil's interview with Rick King for the film* Voices in Wartime.

~

Iwas born in Bogota, Colombia in 1962 in the month of the comets. In the Chinese horoscope I am a tiger. These are the monkey years, and usually tigers have a very slow difficult time in a monkey year. I started dancing before walking and right after that I took on poetry.

I just love words and music. My father used to play a lot of music while I was in the womb. He always played music. I think that I picked up on the rhythms. We talk in Colombia like Italians, very fast and when we talk we look like we are fighting. But we're not; we're just talking.

I left Colombia out of some kind of strange destiny, because I had to be here today. One thing, I was always glancing a little bit ahead into the future, reading the signs around me. I knew that if I stayed I would have to go to the mountains because I would probably get disappeared eventually. Deep inside me I saw no other way. I had this great feeling of running and running and running away. So that's what I did.

Like a puzzle, I started placing the pieces one by one until I just got out. I went to Miami just to check it out for vacation

—I had to believe it was a vacation. It has become the longest vacation. Before I left Colombia, I remember looking at every bird, every tree, every street, at faces, houses, buildings, and I knew I was saying good-bye for a very long time. I knew that I would never leave otherwise.

It's as if I left because I wanted to stay. That was a way of surviving beyond and before it happened. I saw it coming and I said that I was not going to let it happen.

The Endless Civil War

The conflict in Colombia started a very long time ago, more than 50 years ago. Colombia is a very rich country. It's one of the richest countries in its biodiversity. It has a lot of petroleum, 24-karat gold, and emeralds. It has very rich soil. You throw down a seed and the next thing you see is a tree with very sweet, wonderful fruit.

It's a country with a very long history of corrupted governments. All the rich land and all the opportunities are in the hands of very few. You can just handle so much humiliation and hunger and lack of opportunities. What do you do with all these frustrations, wanting to do what we would be able to do in a normal environment?

People have to fight for their rights and have to fight for justice. Until social justice is achieved in Colombia you can kill everyone and the situation is not going to change. Hunger and injustice is like the sun; you can't just put your finger up to block it and then try to say it's not there. It will always be there until justice is done.

The conflict in Colombia is very complicated. In the beginning, it was about people with few opportunities fighting against government corruption. Then the middle and upper classes that own all the land needed people to defend them, so along came a group called the paramilitary. The government is suspected of having ties to the paramilitary. The military, like other militaries in Latin America, created a plan like Condor in Chile to erase whole generations of younger people that had ideas about where the country should go.

Whole generations in Argentina and Chile, in Peru, in Ecuador, in Bolivia, in Paraguay and Uruguay and Colombia disappeared. Then the narco traffickers came into the picture and are now suspected of having ties to parts of the government. The guerrillas are suspected of having ties to the narco traffickers—not all of them, but enough to make the fight very complex, because then you lose your objective, your reason.

I understand that the guerrillas defend the poorest people, the people who have been taken advantage of for over 100 years. Those are the people that they're defending and they're defending the land from the corruption. But then where do you draw the line? It's very complex. It's almost like we had our own Vietnam War in Colombia.

Memory and Return

When I went back to Colombia, I started asking friends, people I knew, about the disappearance of my brother. I found myself not only asking about my brother Pedro but asking, "Where is Julieta? Where is Chaparro? Where is Juan? Where is Maria? Where is Madalene? Where is . . ."

I was afraid to ask. I was very afraid to ask because the answer was always the same. Looking back at the numbers we realized it was a whole generation. It was very hard to ask.

It was, "So-and-so was tired of the corruption and what was going on and they took up arms and went to the mountains. Or he was taken by the paramilitary. Or he's in jail. Oh, her, she's . . . we don't know. She disappeared. Oh, she went to the corner just to buy bread and never came back. Oh, last time we saw him was at a party and these men that came in a car and took him and we don't see him any more." "Oh, and where is so and so?" "Oh, well, I think he's somewhere in a country very far away." Suddenly a whole generation I knew was not there— they were all away or lost.

The political situation I grew up in affects my writing, and I write about social content a lot. I also write about love. But when I write about love, even an erotic poem, I speak of something that exists within a social context.

I think that we are individuals, but we are also a collective, a community. Everything that has to do with social issues influences our individual lives. Love, the things we see, regular daily life, is all influenced by what's going on around you. How you make your bread, how you speak of something, you cannot get away from it. That affects our individuality and for me it's very important to speak of that place where you can be an individual with taste and eccentricities and whatever.

The poem "Letter To the Brother That Went to War" had a different title: "What December 1990 Brought Us." It's a poem written to my brother. Then when this war came upon us, I changed the title because other people were also seeing what is happening in Colombia. Suddenly it was not only my brother—when I looked closely it was a whole generation that was disappearing. We're just now looking at the numbers.

I'm very close to my brother. Pedro is his name, Pedro Villamil. I came to the United States in 1984, and I promised him I was going to take him with me a little bit later. I struggled here in the United States, coming to a new country, to a completely different culture and a completely different language. For a poet, that was a lot to take. Then I had to start putting it off and putting it off.

I didn't see my brother for eight years. In the ninth year I lost him to disappearance. Disappearance means we don't know where, we don't know how, we just don't know. He went out one day, like anybody else, and never came back. He had no reason to leave. No reason. He just never came back.

I have dreams about him and it's very, very hard. I think that one of the things that people cannot ever recover from is disappearance. Not knowing what happened. Not having a place to mourn.

My mother, Alicia, she's a very fervent Catholic. She never wanted to give a mass in the church for him. We told her we probably ought to have a place in the cemetery for Pedro but she refused. She said, oh no, Pedro's coming, Pedro is coming one day.

He would never have left my mother. Pedro was the kind of son that a mother dreams of. Momma what do you want? Oh, Momma this and Momma that. Always making her laugh, helping her in the kitchen. Oh, Momma you want this, but it broke, so I'll fix it, don't worry.

Pedro was never going to leave. He was 32-years old when he disappeared. He was the light of the house, the light of my mother's eyes.

In the poem "My Name is Pedro" he is a symbol of all the people disappeared in Central and South American countries. Pedro died of this disappearance and it's not like other people you know who died of cancer, or of AIDS, which is terrible. People who die suddenly, who go to sleep and never wake up, so you can say he died of this or he died of that. But when you don't know, when you don't find a place to go to mourn that loss, what did they die of?

That's why I said Pedro died of disappearance. He is in the long list of people that disappear every day in Central and South American countries.

I feel like I'm talking to my brother every time I write about him. It's a way of communicating with him, with his memory, with what could have been. With the idea of not seeing him getting older with me and knowing his children and his wife. He never got a chance to have a wife or children. That was always what I imagined it was going to be like.

Taking a Stand

The war in Iraq made it feel very personal because I saw in it the pattern of the unfortunate foreign policy of the United States being repeated. With this war in Iraq, I knew many innocent people were going to be killed for something that from the beginning was a lie.

I was very worried and uneasy thinking that a country can go to another country and just basically take away, by means of lying, their riches, which is oil. That's what happened in Colombia.

I took to the streets. I took to all the possibilities. I went to A.N.S.W.E.R., I went to meetings with Not in Our Name, with Latinos Against the War. My husband, Carlos, is an organizer in the community and so we started organizing. We did a big march in East L.A. We went to all the marches that we could. Immediately we mobilized, we talked to everyone.

Prior to the war in Iraq was 9/11, and we were left for a few months with our mouths open thinking it just could not be true. It could not happen here. How could this danger that was created by the United States in another country just suddenly land here? It was not possible. It was like the nightmare was repeating itself. I felt like I was back on a street in Colombia, a street in some Third World country. How could it be happening here?

Then everything started building up, building up, building up, building up to the war in Iraq. It was one mistake and one overlaying of wording and reasons after the other. It was unbelievable. You were seeing these big, fat, unreal lies being built in front of our own noses and we couldn't do anything about it. We felt so impotent.

There's a saying that if you speak to the ceiling it'll come down on you. I said I could not believe that we're being dragged into this heavy karma. How long did we think we could get away with it?

Since the war in Iraq, I've been writing a lot. I had all these poems about my brother and other poems about Colombia. I wrote something about Hiroshima and different experiences of war and what it does to people in their normal little places. We try to express ourselves and what is coming down on other people who can't even cry. It's all coming so fast but we are witnesses and how can we not write that?

So I started writing and I started communicating with a lot of people through the Internet, and the news came that we're doing this, we're doing that. So I sent "My Name is Pedro" to Poets Against the War, but it's directly linked to all the work that we've been doing to protest this war.

Sending the poem to Poets Against the War and knowing the stand that the poets took made me feel better. But I knew that even if we could not stop the war, this is the place where poets should be. I felt proud and I felt this is the kind of thing that we should be doing, even if I knew at that point this war was going to happen. What we were doing was part of something bigger.

All the machinery put into creating this war did not start a few months ago or since September 11. It started way before that, as a consequence of many accumulating things. I knew that once the machine reached that point, it was just letting the people know that this is going to happen despite whatever you do.

Whatever you do, it's going to happen. That was very clear. For us it was just a way of telling people what was happening, a way of saying no. This is what we should be doing, saying no.

The Poet as Witness

Poets are the critics of feelings and experience. We do pretty much what the mathematicians do with numbers, but we do it with language. Poetry for me is at the foundation of culture.

At this moment, we are speaking of poetry but we're also recording. We're recording a memory of the human experience that will last a long time. That memory has to be put into words first, of image and color, and then our human experience takes off to a place in time and permanence.

I think poets are witnesses in charge of making human experience permanent. One of the funny things about poetry is that you will never see a bestseller poet. Maybe, after 50 to 100 years, you can make it into the news, like Neruda. So I'll be very lucky if people hear a little bit of what comes through me.

Children, for the poet, are the eyes into the future. You cannot help but to realize that what you are writing, even though it may sometimes sound wordy or complicated or deep or dense, you're writing for that child. I hope they'll be reading that when they're 40 or 50. I've seen poems change people's lives.

The role of the poet everywhere, not only in the United States but also in the rest of America, is to be the conscience of the culture, of the community; not only by writing, but also by reading. There are a lot of young poets performing their poetry now because we have mass communication such as radio and movies. That seems to be getting people to listen to poets.

It is a challenge, but I think that poets resort to all kinds of media. We collaborate with painters, with musicians, with dancers, with film people. So there is this active, organic life of the writer and the poet within the community.

I don't think that enough people in the United States are aware of what's going on. People are a little more aware lately with the help of technology like e-mail and digital cameras that can capture certain realities, but there are a lot of things that still seem like well-kept secrets.

For example, a lot of people don't know that we have a School of the Americas in Texas, which provides training to very high officials in the military who go all over Latin America. I hope that more people will get to know because it is important and it is America.

America goes all the way to the Tierra del Fuego. Central America, Mexico is America. Colombia is America. If we don't take care of the fire in our neighbor's house, our brother's house, it's only a matter of time until it starts raining fire on our heads.

Letter to the Brother That Went to War

/

Antonieta Villamil

What can I tell you
dear brother
mutilated in silence.

You disappear,
as so many of
my brothers, with
rigorous synchronicity.

The dripping of the clock
coagulates my eyes.

Between brows and eye-corner glances
I keep an ash
that repels the fire
that doesn't find your bones.

A tomb I know by heart
butchers my hands.

With the only effort
I have left
I write these lines,

while outside
and around us
everything collapses
and bleeds.

Part 3:
LOOKING BACK

Alix Wilber is a Seattle-based novelist and co-executive producer for the documentary film Voices in Wartime. *She also co-produced the short documentary film* Beyond Wartime.

Why Art, Why Now

Alix Wilber

Recently, we received an email at *voicesinwartime.org* from a gentleman who wrote in response to our focus on art in a time of war: "Poetry? Sorry, but it seems so thin!"

He has a point—certainly the pens of poets such as Wilfred Owen and Federico Garcia Lorca proved no match for the mighty guns that cut them down. So why did they write—Owen from the trenches of World War I, Lorca in defiance of the Spanish fascists who eventually murdered him? Their poetry neither saved their lives nor ended war, and fame is of little interest to the dead. One could argue that the beauty of the poetry they produced was reason enough for them to have written it, but that is evaluating the quality of their work in terms of its value as art to the greater society; it still doesn't explain the compulsion of the individual poets to create it.

And it doesn't embrace the finger-paintings of children traumatized by genocide; the clumsy verses written by ordinary people with no pretensions to art—work scribbled hastily on flimsy paper in response to extraordinary feelings of anguish and despair.

In his *Ethics*, the philosopher Spinoza wrote: " . . . suffering ceases to be suffering as soon as we form a clear and precise picture of it." And perhaps this is the crux of the matter: perhaps we expect too much of art if we ask it to prevent violence: no pen is mightier than a machete in the act of separating a head from its body; the words of the poet are inevitably drowned out in the roar of the mob. Perhaps the most we can hope for is that after the blood-letting is over, art allows us to look back and understand what we have experienced.

"My subject is War, and the pity of War," Wilfred Owen wrote in the planned preface of a volume of poetry he never lived to see in print. "The Poetry is in the pity. Yet these elegies are to this generation in no sense consolatory. They may be to the next. All a poet can do today is warn. That is why the true Poets must be truthful."

I think Owen sells himself—and his poetry—short, however, when he says his elegies are in no sense consolatory to the generation of young men who experienced the events he wrote about. It is true that for many years immediately following The Great War, Owen's work and that of the other war poets was not popular—was, for the most part, ignored and, when noticed at all, denigrated as anti-patriotic whining. And yet in the days when post-traumatic stress disorder (PTSD) was known as "shell-shock" and was a source of shame to the many who suffered from it, we have no way of knowing how many of Owen's contemporaries found private consolation in having their own traumas confirmed by the record of suffering he left behind.

Some scientists say that language is the very thing that makes us human, and yet, any parakeet can learn to talk. What differentiates us from the rest of the animal kingdom is not the ability to produce language, but rather the compulsion to use it—and not just to communicate basic needs or information, but rather to go beyond and express the ineffable. From the cave paintings at Lescaux to Picasso's *Guernica*; from *The Iliad* to *Dulce et Decorum Est*, this expressive impulse reflects what is essentially human: the need to commemorate what is meaningful in our lives and pass it on to future generations through the stories we leave behind.

It took 50,000 years, give or take a millennium or two, from the earliest origins of language to the invention of Gutenberg's revolutionary printing press. Now, a mere five centuries later, we stand at the dawn of the 21st century—and yet, *plus ça change, plus c'est la meme chose*: wars still rage; ethnic and religious hatreds blaze hot; somewhere in the world, a new Troy burns every day.

"Few things arouse stronger emotions than love and war," historian Jon Stallworthy remarks in one of the interviews we include in this book, "and while one might expect that in time of war the emotion would be hate, that is not always the case." This sentiment is given fuller examination by the renowned psychiatrist, holocaust survivor and writer, Viktor Frankl, whose book, *Man's Search for Meaning*, is a remarkable meditation on both the horror and despair of war, and the power of hope to transcend it. Of his time in the Nazi camps, Frankl wrote:

"We had to learn ourselves, and furthermore, we had to teach the despairing men, that it did not really matter what we expected from life, but rather what life expected from us. We had to stop asking about the meaning of life, and instead to think of ourselves as those who were being questioned by life—daily and hourly—the meaning of life differs from man to man, and from moment to moment."

Elsewhere in his book, Frankl writes that even in a concentration camp, each individual still has choices to make every moment, every day—if only the choice of in what manner he or she will meet suffering and death. "Man can preserve a vestige of spiritual freedom, of independence of mind," he states, "even in such terrible conditions of psychic and physical stress."

For Frankl, one of the things that kept him alive was the determination to reconstruct a book manuscript the Nazis had seized and destroyed—a work he felt that he, and he alone, was qualified to write; if he perished in the camps, the book would perish too—and with it the unique perspective of the one irreplaceable individual who had been Viktor Frankl.

Psychiatrist and author Jonathan Shay tells us that "[n]arrative is central to recovery from severe trauma. It's not simply the telling of the story, it is the whole social process. If I have suffered some terrible experience, I have to be socially empowered to tell the story. You have to be socially empowered to hear it. The final step that closes the loop—and this is one place where artists have played a role from the beginning of time—is to retell the story to others."

In a world where, increasingly, entire societies—soldiers and civilians alike—are the victims of war and trauma, this process becomes more essential than ever. And Shay points out that while the artist can play a role in any or all of the steps of communalization, it isn't necessary for him or her to have been an actual trauma survivor or to have personally witnessed it in order to be a faithful recorder of its emotional essence. It's enough that the retelling contains enough of the truth so that the person who experiences it says ,"'Yes, you were listening, you heard, you heard at least some of it. And you retold it with the truthfulness, with the emotion, that I can recognize.'"

The physician and essayist Lewis Thomas wrote, "We pass the word around; we ponder how the case is put by different people, we read the poetry; we meditate over the literature; we play the music; we change our minds; we reach an understanding. Society evolves this way, not by shouting each other down, but by the unique capacity of unique, individual human beings to comprehend each other."

Which brings us back to the comment from the gentleman who wrote us: "Poetry? Sorry, but it seems so thin." True, but sometimes it's all we have standing between us and annihilation of the soul.

Wilfred Owen, *a British soldier-poet during the First World War, died in combat a week before the Allies and Germans signed the Armistice in 1918. His story and two of his poems are featured in the documentary film* Voices in Wartime. *The following poem was published posthumously in 1920.*

Strange Meeting

Wilfred Owen

It seemed that out of battle I escaped
Down some profound dull tunnel, long since scooped
Through granites which titanic wars had groined.
Yet also there encumbered sleepers groaned,
Too fast in thought or death to be bestirred.
Then, as I probed them, one sprang up, and stared
With piteous recognition in fixed eyes,
Lifting distressful hands as if to bless.
And by his smile, I knew that sullen hall,
By his dead smile I knew we stood in Hell.
With a thousand pains that vision's face was grained;
Yet no blood reached there from the upper ground,
And no guns thumped, or down the flues made moan.
"Strange friend," I said, "here is no cause to mourn."
"None," said that other, "save the undone years,
The hopelessness. Whatever hope is yours,
Was my life also; I went hunting wild
After the wildest beauty in the world,
Which lies not calm in eyes, or braided hair,
But mocks the steady running of the hour.
And if it grieves, grieves richlier than here.

For of my glee might many men have laughed,

And of my weeping something had been left,

Which must die now. I mean the truth untold,

The pity of war, the pity war distilled.

Now men will go content with what we spoiled,

Or, discontent, boil bloody, and be spilled.

They will be swift with swiftness of the tigress.

None will break ranks, though nations trek from progress.

Courage was mine, and I had mystery.

Wisdom was mine, and I had mastery:

To miss the march of this retreating world

Into vain citadels that are not walled.

Then, when much blood had clogged their chariot-wheels,

I would go up and wash them from sweet wells,

Even with truths that lie too deep for taint.

I would have poured my spirit without stint

But not through wounds; not on the cess of war.

Foreheads of men have bled where no wounds were.

I am the enemy you killed, my friend.

I knew you in this dark: for so you frowned

Yesterday through me as you jabbed and killed.

I parried; but my hands were loath and cold.

Let us sleep now—

Dominic Hibberd is the author of Wilfred Owen: A New Biography *and several other books about poets and poetry of the First World War. He lives in the United Kingdom. The following narrative was adapted from Hibberd's interview with Rick King for the film* Voices in Wartime.

Wilfred Owen and *Siegfried Sassoon* were British soldiers, among the most well-known poets of the First World War, and close friends and colleagues. Owen died in an ill-fated assault on a German position at the end of the war. Sassoon lived on after the war until 1967.

Thirty Days on the Front Line: Sassoon and Owen

Dominic Hibberd

Wilfred Owen was a poet who was steeped in poetry. He'd read a great deal of poetry in many different periods—not just the Romantics, although they were always the most important poets for him. When he wrote poetry, he used all the literary talents he could get hold of. A poem like "Strange Meeting," for example, is full of all sorts of extraordinary echoes. It has traces of Arthurian legend, Spencer, Milton, Shakespeare, Keats, and all sorts of others. There are remarkable sound effects and most elaborate lines, but also wonderfully simple lines put in together.

"Strange Meeting" is about the First World War. It's a scene in a dugout, but at the same time it's about myth and human experience in all ages. He sets it in some unspecified time and is very careful to avoid pinning it down to, say, 1914 or 1918. One line, for example, was "I was a German conscript, and your friend." Owen changed that to "I am the enemy you killed, my friend," because he didn't want that reference to Germany or even to conscription. Owen wanted to get the poem into a universal context, which you can do through literature and poetry more than any other medium.

It's interesting that Owen sent his last finished poem "Spring

Offensive," unfinished, to Sassoon and said, "Is this worth going on with? I don't want to write anything to which a soldier would say 'No Compris!' He wanted to be understood by ordinary soldiers and by children. He particularly was anxious to write for future generations.

I've met so many people who have come up to me after lectures and said, "Wilfred Owen is the first poet I really find exciting. I read him in school, but I've never forgotten, and I've gone on admiring him always." To some extent, that's new. My mother, for example, who lived through the First World War as a child, always said she couldn't read Wilfred Owen at all and didn't need to because she knew what war was like anyway. It was just too horrible for her and too moving, and it reminded her too much of the suffering that everybody had gone through, and she didn't want to know about it.

It was the next generation, my generation, that really began to wake up to Owen, I think. And then another generation in the 1960s, at the time of the Vietnam War—Owen's poetry was just the kind of thing they wanted. So he became a national figure in the way he hadn't been before. And his reputation has gone on growing in the most astonishing way.

During Wilfred Owen's lifetime, five of his poems were published, but really only three of them any place where anybody would have noticed. He was totally unknown except to a handful of literary people. It wasn't until after his death that his poems began to be known. There was an article published, for example, at the end of the war about the great poets of the war. Sassoon is a major figure in that article and gets a full-page portrait; Owen isn't mentioned. Owen isn't mentioned in most books about First World War literature until perhaps the mid-1920s, and then he's still a figure that literary people know, but nobody else much knows. His reputation takes off very slowly. Now, of course, he's regarded, by far and away, as the greatest of the First World War poets, but that was not so at all at the time.

Owen was lucky in yet another way, in that he spent a long time in England recuperating from shell shock, so he had plenty of time to write. By the spring of 1918, he was ready to put his poems together as a book. He had somebody in London, who he hoped would find a publisher. In the end, that never happened. He drafted a preface for us, and so all we have is one scrappy little fragment of paper with a lot of it crossed out; it's so very much a preliminary draft. But it's clear from that and from the list of poems that goes with it, that every poem has a motive or reason. He had a fairly clear intent to wake people up, shock people through vivid description and satire and make them feel what he called "the pity of War." Not protest—that was a stage he went through—but the ultimate thing was to feel pity, because that meant that you were genuinely sympathizing with the ordinary soldier. You were putting yourself in the position of a soldier in the front line. That is what poetry is for— to enable readers to put themselves into the position of other people and sympathize with human predicaments.

Owen says quite clearly in his preface that he's not going to use proper names. He did think, even right to the end, that Germany had to be defeated, that this was the only outcome that could put that war to an end. But he felt that it was desperately important to remember the Germans were human beings, and the vast majority of them were much like us: well-intentioned, not all-out to kill and dominate the world. Only a few top generals were like that. Owen tried to make his poetry appeal to anybody on any side and of any nationality.

It's interesting that his poems have recently been translated into German, apparently very successfully. I myself lectured in Germany once or twice and found that the audiences were tremendously appreciative and interested. They can appreciate his poems just as much as we can.

Owen's Life Before Meeting Sassoon

Wilfred Owen came from a lower-middle-class background. His father was a railway official, a stationmaster for awhile, and then monsignor. He never earned very much money, but he earned as much as, say, a schoolteacher. He had four children to be brought up, so there was never any spare cash around.

Wilfred Owen's mother was a very pious evangelical, and I think the father was probably also more religious than is generally believed. So Wilfred had a strong religious background. He went to some quite decent schools, not outstanding ones, but he received a reasonable education. Some of the teachers took a great interest in him and helped him. He wanted very much to go to university, but I don't think he ever would have done that; his parents couldn't have afforded it, and he wasn't quite clever enough to get a scholarship.

Everything in Owen's life reappears in the poetry somehow. You have to remember that he was not only a poet and a soldier, but also a qualified teacher. He wrote teaching poems. I think he wanted us to understand, to know, to learn. He was also an evangelical who spent more than a year as an assistant in an evangelical parish. So he knew how to get a message across. He was preaching poetry and teaching poetry. He was committed to being the three things that he was: poet, teacher, soldier.

Owen was a great admirer or Keats and other romantics, Wordsworth in particular, and he knew from them that to be a poet was the greatest calling that anybody could possibly have. But, of course, poetry wouldn't make him any money, so he planned to be a teacher. And he wanted, if possible, to be a teacher in the secondary system because it paid much better.

When the war broke out, Owen was working as a tutor in France for a family in the Pyrenees. The happiest month of his life was probably August 1914. France had conscription, so there was no recruiting propaganda, and he wasn't under pressure. He didn't feel that he had to rush and join the army in the way that so many young men in England did. He said that he felt his duty really was to stay alive, because poets were needed.

As the war went on, he returned to England and began to feel the pressure of the recruiting campaign, and he realized that he really ought to have joined the army like everybody else. He finally did so in October 1915. By that stage, many of the volunteers had already volunteered. This was a last burst before conscription was introduced. He was, in the end, quite enthusiastic to join, but for a long time, perhaps almost a year, he was content to stay in France and keep his own life alive and not feel that he had to go and get himself killed.

Owen wanted to be an officer from the beginning. But he hadn't been to the right school, so he was lucky that he did finally find a way in. The army was prepared to regard him as a gentleman because he'd been abroad for awhile. So that gave him the social status that he'd never quite had before. He went into the Artists' Rifles, which was a training regiment that produced enormous numbers of officers for the army during the war. He had a very high-powered, efficient training. By the time he emerged, he was a very capable young officer. He then joined the Manchester Regiment in the summer of 1916 as a fully trained officer, a second lieutenant.

Becoming an officer put him in the right rank, and he joined early enough not to be seen as what came to be known as a temporary gentleman. Later in the war, so many people came up from the ranks to be officers that they quite clearly weren't in the same social class, but Owen avoided that. Owen had had a rather good time in England as a trainee officer. He had done well, he was highly regarded, and he didn't have to suffer any particular discomforts. He was sent out to France at the beginning of 1917, and within three weeks, he was in one of the most appalling circumstances imaginable.

He went into a German dugout in no man's land that had recently been captured as a British outpost. He had to keep his platoon there for 50 hours under constant shellfire, expecting at any minute to be buried alive. The place was slowly flooding with rainwater, rising above their knees. It was an unspeakably horrific experience, and it colored everything that happened to him thereafter. But in a strange kind of way, he had already written about aspects of this experience in his poetry. He'd had nightmares of this kind before. There are earlier poems with lines that pretty accurately describe what he was in.

Next his platoon was taken out of that dugout for a short period, and put back in again in quite a different situation, on the top of a hill in very hard frost. They were out on the snow exposed, unable to move. One man in his platoon froze to death. They all might have died of thirst because the water froze in their water bottles. Then his battalion moved farther south into a fresh sector of the line where there hadn't been much fighting before. They hadn't dug any trenches, so they were very vulnerable to shellfire. Owen was eventually almost killed by a shell that dropped near his head while he was asleep, and he was blown into the air. That finally broke his nerve, but his nerve had been going for some time under the strain of it all.

After all, it was an utterly alien experience for a man of his background. He'd worked in a parish, he'd been a teacher, but he'd never been anywhere near fighting or gunfire or shell explosions.

That was unimaginable for him, as it was, of course, for the great majority of soldiers. Finally, in April 1917, his nerve broke, and he had to be sent back to England. That was considered to be a disgrace by a lot of people in the army. They didn't really understand shell shock. The doctors understood it, but the average senior officer didn't. There is some evidence that Owen was accused of cowardice by his temporary commanding officer. That would have been a terrible blow and the final straw that broke him.

I have heard it said that Owen was very lucky not to have been court-martialed, but I think that's absolute nonsense. The army was actually very sensible with him and sent him to a good hospital just outside Edinburgh: Craiglockhart Hospital, a place that treated shell-shocked officers. There, he was put under the care of the ideal doctor, exactly the man he needed, someone who understood him—strange man with odd, highly unusual ideas. Owen was put through a kind of a sociological training. He was made to reconnect with his environment by studying the locality. It worked. It was marvelously successful. Within a few months, he was very nearly right again.

Now that Owen was almost well from shell shock, he had another enormous piece of luck: Siegfried Sassoon was sent to the same hospital, supposedly as a patient, though really just to shut him up, because Sassoon had protested against the war. The authorities didn't want to court-martial him, so they pretended that he was shell shocked even though he wasn't.

So suddenly Sassoon and Owen were in the same hospital together. Owen plucked up his courage, went to introduce himself to the senior man, and they became good friends. Owen very rapidly discovered how Sassoon had been writing and what Sassoon's political attitude to the war was. He picked it up and began writing himself.

Sassoon: Poet, Mad Bomber, Protester

Sassoon came from a nearly upper-class background. He'd been to Cambridge. He had money. He had influential friends. He belonged to an entirely different sort of world from Owen, but he was like Owen—bookish and dedicated to poetry—so that gave them something immediately in common.

In 1916, Sassoon had begun to protest against the war with some encouragement from friends at home. Finally, he decided that he would make a serious public protest and get it publicized. He composed it with the help of civilian pacifists. His soldier friends, most of them anyway, thought he was mad. It was the civilians who persuaded him that he should act as he did. He made a very strong public statement against the war that got read in the House of Commons. The authorities had to do something, and so they decided that the best thing to do was to put him away in a shell shock hospital until he behaved properly.

Sassoon had a divided personality, in a way. He was a poet on the one hand, and on the other hand, he was a bit of a dilettante. Before the war, he was tremendously keen on fox hunting and cricket, and his sporting self seemed to dominate. But before the war broke out, he eventually decided that he would make himself a poet and concentrate on that side. Then the war came, and for him, as for so many people, it was a resolution. It gave him the chance to set aside his own personal problems and take up a bigger cause. He joined up a few days before the war broke out, in the [Sussex] Yeomanry. For a while, he was an ordinary-rank private soldier on horseback, but that didn't last for very long, partly because he was thrown by a horse and broke his arm. He then decided he would, after all, become an officer in a main regiment.

Sassoon never had the really bad experiences that Owen had. Each of them, I think, spent about 30 days in the front line. He was in the war for longer, but he was never in those extreme front-line situations that Owen was in. Nevertheless, he came very near to shell shock, and he recognized that he was very close to a breakdown by the time he came out of the line. But he had long periods of recovery at home, and he was not under the same kind of strain in the front line.

Sassoon was foolhardy. I don't think you'd call him brave. He did silly things and was almost certainly regarded as unreliable by his seniors. He was held back on a number of occasions when he really ought to have been in the fighting. He was extraordinarily reckless, and did on one occasion capture a trench single-handedly. He was called Mad Jack, as a number of officers were.

Sassoon did go through a period of being frenziedly anti-German —a very short period when his closest friend in the army was killed. Sassoon attended the burial, and then felt he ought to take revenge.

For a while, he was ferocious and did what he could to kill Germans, although, of course, the Germans were out of sight in the trenches, so he never really knew whether he'd killed one or not. But it didn't last very long. It was a sort of battle frenzy that soldiers in history have sometimes. So even Sassoon got it, but then he was ashamed of himself and calmed down.

Sassoon started publishing poetry at his own expense well before the war. He produced a number of little volumes of no great value. But he had published quite a bit by the time he met Owen, so he was relatively well known. His book *The Old Huntsman and Other Poems*, which was the first book of his that Owen read, contained a number of very powerful war poems and satires against the war. These were unlike anything that anybody else had written at that stage, or at any rate, that anybody had published. They shook Owen considerably. He was deeply moved by them.

Sassoon's poems were regarded by reviewers at the time as being more like epigrams than poems. And they're certainly more like epigrams than Owen's poems are—they're short, punchy, satirical. They were designed to be put at the foot of a column in a magazine so that they kicked you in the stomach instantly. His aim was to shock civilians into realizing what the war was really like. So he tried to describe actual incidents at the front in simple, raw, vivid language, with the ultimate hope that the civilians who read them would then bring pressure to bear on the politicians. The politicians would then negotiate a diplomatic solution to the war, and actually do it through talking instead of fighting. Civilians at the time believed that was a possibility in 1917, but I think historians would now say that actually it wasn't a possibility: that it was a hopeless hope.

The tone of Sassoon's poems certainly is bitter, some of them more so than others. His essential skill, he felt, was actually in writing in a lyrical, elegiac way rather than a satirical way. As the pressure of war experience slackened in him, his poems lost their satirical edge, but for a while he was deeply anxious that people at home should know what it was like to be stuck in those trenches being shot at day after day, what it was like to die slowly of agonizing wounds.

Sassoon and Owen at Craiglockhart Hospital

Sassoon was rather bored by newcomers. He didn't really want to meet anybody else while he was at Craiglockhart. He was ashamed of being there anyway. He felt he was a failure. He felt he'd been silenced by authority, and that he shouldn't have given in. So he wasn't terribly enthusiastic when Owen knocked on his door

Owen, on the other hand, was immensely excited to meet a published poet who was writing a new sort of poetry. He kept up his visits, and they did eventually become close friends. Owen quickly learned Sassoon's political view of the war: that it could be brought to an end by diplomatic meetings. That it wasn't necessary to go on and on fighting until everybody was killed. That the politicians could sit around a table and actually talk to the Germans, and that the Germans had shown some interest in peace negotiations, too.

So Owen picked that up very quickly, and when you have a political basis for protesting against a war, you can start writing about it. If you think that the war is the right thing and a noble cause, as everybody did in 1914, and as Owen himself thought right up to early 1917, then you don't protest against it. That would be ridiculous. You just want to get it finished as soon as possible. You don't talk about its horrors because you know they're there— you just have to put up with them and live or die with them as best you can. But if your political view changes and you think that the war could be brought to an end by the politicians, then you start writing against it. So Owen's poems at Craiglockhart are very much in Sassoon's style. The influence of Sassoon is strong. Owen took manuscripts to Sassoon, asked for advice, and got advice. The poems were no doubt improved as a result, but we don't know very much about how that happened, because there isn't that much manuscript evidence to show what Sassoon's interventions were.

Sassoon also helped Owen on a psychological level. Owen knew he was gay from quite early on. He learned that Sassoon was also gay and was willing to talk about it. And that, I think, helped Owen enormously. By the last year of his life Owen was far more confident and at ease with himself than he had been before, although he never suffered quite the same agonies of conscience that Sassoon perhaps did.

Sassoon quite quickly recognized, according to Sassoon's own records, at any rate, that Owen was a better poet than he was, and that there maybe wasn't much that he could teach him. But he certainly encouraged him, and gave him contacts in London, and hoped that he would get published. Sassoon's friend Robert Graves came up to see him at Craiglockhart and also met Owen. Graves was actually more enthusiastic than Sassoon and more convinced that Owen really was a poet. So between them, they introduced Owen to people in London who might have been able to get him published. But they also saw that he was still in the early stages, still feeling his way. So they, and Owen too, felt that there should be no great hurry in getting him published. He had to find his own feet first.

The pressure of meeting Sassoon got Owen writing at an extraordinary pace. He was remarkably productive in that one year between meeting Sassoon and going back to the front line and soon after that being killed. I suppose he wrote 30 or 40 poems about the war that will always be remembered.

Crossing the Canal

If you're going to send young men into battle, it's no good pretending that it's a great crusade and a wonderful adventure, that this is some glorious thing, and that it's sweet and decorous to die for one's country in battle. It's none of those things. It's terrible and unspeakable.

The last battle that Owen was in, which was also the last battle of the First World War and the final victory that persuaded Germany to drop out and give up, was a very important event and not just the ending of a squabble. It was the crossing of the Sambre-Oise Canal in France. In most cases along the British front, that crossing was carried out with great success and not very much loss of life. But in one place, or maybe two, the crossing troops ran into severe trouble. The Germans had more artillery ahead than had been recognized, and there was absolutely no shelter.

Engineers working for Wilfred's battalion built a bridge across the canal with enormous skill, in half an hour. Some men got across, and then it was smashed by a shell. They had to still keep on trying to reconstruct this thing and get more people to cross. It seems likely that Owen was actually on a raft when he was hit and killed. Rafts had certainly been constructed for this operation to get men and materials out to the bridge to carry on with the repairs. We have no idea whether he was hit by shrapnel, machine gun bullets, or a rifle, nor whether he died instantly or not until some hours later. So the ending of his life is a mystery.

The message got back to Shrewsbury, where his parents were, on the actual day of the Armistice. It is said that the bells were actually ringing to celebrate the Armistice when the telegram arrived at his parents' house. His father had been out at work, and his mother, who adored him, went to open the telegram and got the terrible news. She never really recovered. He was her first-born and the child she loved most. And he was so nearly a survivor. The war was over. He ought to have survived.

That canal crossing was called off, perhaps only ten minutes after he was killed. It was a matter of minutes, that's all. It sounds awful to say so, but in a way he was lucky even in that, because his early death is part of what has kept his reputation so powerful and moving. If he lived to be 90, it would have been a very different story.

Jon Stallworthy is a professor at the University of Oxford, an expert on war poetry. He is also the author of a biography of Wilfred Owen and editor of The Oxford Book of War Poetry. *This narrative was adapted from Stallworthy's interview with Rick King for the film* Voices in Wartime.

A History of Poetry and War

Jon Stallworthy

Few things arouse stronger emotions than love and war, and while one might expect that in time of war the emotion would be hate, that is not always the case. People—soldiers—express affection for the people they've left behind: their wives, their children, their comrades, their country. The power in many of the best war poems derives from the driving power of the emotion behind it.

Heroes and Ordinary Men

The poetry of war starts with the Old Testament and with *The Iliad*, and then it goes through to *The Aeneid*. When it first reaches the shores of what is now England, Anglo-Saxon poetry has the same sort of chivalric code. You are reading about the brave actions of heroes who are almost all of noble birth. They are normally horsemen, and their business is fighting; that's what they do. This ethos continues through the Norman Conquest when the language undergoes its wonderful mutation.

Anglo-Saxon literature, Anglo-Saxon language, is very gritty and specific, with lots of short, tough words. When it meets the long, resonant, polysyllables of Anglo-Norman—of Norman-French—you get this wonderful confluence of two languages, making the English that we now speak. And with the French element comes a highly sophisticated cultural tradition in which there are many long, heroic poems, like the *Chanson de Roland*,

and a whole code of honor and military virtues as exemplified by a wide range of heroes.

The first major author in what we now think of as English would be Chaucer, who was a soldier. Chaucer writes "The Knight's Tale," which tells of one of these elegant, heroic, gentlemanly knights on horseback whose son is a squire, also on horseback. The poets who follow him—a surprising number, actually—were themselves soldiers. John Donne fought in two expeditions. You have the cavalier poets—the word cavalier coming from "horse" in the chivalric tradition—and Lovelace, famous for his poem "To Lucasta, Going to the Wars":

"True, a new mistress now I chase, the first foe in the field
And with a stronger faith embrace a sword, a horse, a shield."

This continues, and we hear nothing of or from the foot soldiers—the ordinary people who actually would have had to bear the brunt of the battle. But this begins to change by the time of the American Civil War, when in a quite different culture you have most noticeably Walt Whitman, writing in a hospital. And for the first time, the focus is not on heroic actions so much as on the result of actions, heroic or unheroic: wounded people. And when they're wounded, bandaged, and bleeding in a hospital ward, you don't know whether they're aristocrats or foot soldiers.

Whitman went to a hospital to tend to his wounded brother and wrote these wonderful, very moving poems about ordinary soldiers suffering the effects of war. Civil war is always much more painful and uglier than international wars because people are driven by a frenzy to murder their own kind. Something of that extra intensity is, I think, present in Whitman's poems and the work of other very fine poets of the American Civil War.

And then you find this slightly shifting emphasis during the Crimean War in Alfred Lord Tennyson's famous poem, "The Charge of the Light Brigade," where a heroic action is celebrated. He's praising the courage of the soldiers, some of whom are officers and some of whom are just ordinary horsemen, but someone has blundered. There's not an outright endorsement of the action at all. It's a terrible mistake, but the soldiers who have had to live and die with that terrible mistake have shown courage, which he celebrates in the poem.

Then you get to the Boer War, which was the first real war the British had fought for quite a long time. There had been endless frontier campaigns where the British had overwhelming strength and would almost always come home victorious. The Boer War was different. The British Army that sailed for South Africa in 1899 was the first literate army in history. For the first time, the people who can write home and write about what they're enduring are not only the officers but the men too. There's a tremendous outpouring of writing from soldiers and war correspondents in the Boer War: diaries, letters, and lots of poems. The poems almost all sound like Rudyard Kipling, who was a correspondent there and whose poems were already very famous. Kipling at this time and shortly afterward celebrates the achievement of the common soldier.

So, at the beginning of the 20th century, you get this shift in focus from the aristocracy to the ordinary people, which reflects the rise of democracy in western countries. Kipling's poem "Tommy," for example, is a wonderful ringing endorsement of the ordinary common soldier. At the same time Houseman, whose brother was killed in the South African war, writes "The Shropshire Lad" about grenadiers and other soldiers, and celebrates the death of ordinary people. Then, of course, the most famous poem of all is Thomas Hardy's "Drummer Hodge". ("Hodge" is a quintessential English country name.) Hodge is a boy. He's not even a man or a soldier. He's a musician who goes off to a country he has probably never heard of before and is killed in South Africa. Hardy, far from endorsing the undertaking of the war, is intensely aware of the effect that deaths in South Africa have on families in England. In his poems about the soldiers embarking for South Africa, he focuses on the white handkerchiefs waving from the quay as the wives and children see their fathers and husbands going, some of whom will not return. This new focus on ordinary soldiers marks a very important shift.

Homeric Visions, Horrific Realities

The Boer War was over by 1902. Yet only 12 years later, World War I began in Europe. You would have thought that people would have learned the lessons of The Boer War, but they hadn't. Both in

Berlin and in London, there is this extraordinary sort of gaiety and exaltation. In London, crowds were shouting, "To Berlin!" and in Berlin they were shouting, "To London!" Rupert Brooke captured the mood in 1914 with the poem he paradoxically titled "Peace." It begins, "Now God be thanked who has matched us with His hour, and caught our youth, and wakened us from sleeping." He thanks God for the outbreak of war, which has in a sense woken the people up.

Philip Larkin many years later captured the mood beautifully in a poem called "MCMXIV," the Roman numerals standing for 1914. He focused on the queues outside the recruiting offices, with the men grinning as if they're going on holiday. Of course that mood changed most markedly with the Battle of the Somme in July 1916. Up to that point, the first poets of The Great War had had an education that consisted in large measure of study of the classics. Even when I went to school, from 9 a.m. to 11:15 a.m., every child did Latin and/or Greek; and then you did "unimportant" things like history, English, French, and mathematics; the classics were what was central.

Thus that first generation of World War I poets went to war with Homeric expectations. All they knew about war was what they'd read in Virgil, Homer, and Horace. In the early poems—the poems of 1914, 1915—there are no references to bayonets, bullets, or platoons, but hundreds of references to swords, spears, and legions.

Seigfried Sassoon wrote, "We are the happy legion." And a poem written just before the war by Herbert Askwith, called "The Volunteer," has a clerk who has visions of glory in which he is on horseback riding in a great charge with plumes on his helmet, and so on. Rupert Brooke, going to what was going to be Gallipoli, wrote to a friend saying, "Do you think we will stop and make an assault on the plains of Troy?" He was very conscious that Troy was next to Gallipoli. Another poet, Charles Hamilton Sorley, wrote from the western front, "I have not brought my *Odyssey* with me here across the sea." The early poems are full of these references to classical literature and the classical world.

By 1915, most of those poets and those who followed them, came from a quite different cultural background—people who had either no classical education or very little but who were quite widely read in English poetry.

English was not a topic at these schools at that time. You read English in your spare time. One of the curious cultural phenomena of The Great War was that the book more soldiers carried in their pack than any other was Sir Arthur Quiller-Couch's *Oxford Book of English Verse*. On the western front, they sat and read tales of shepherdesses, the seasons, and the natural world amidst a landscape that was utterly blasted and devastated.

This comes through the work of many of the poets, and I think much of the power in the poems is their love for poetry and for the natural world, in addition to their love for the people they'd left behind. They had to live in the awful trenches surrounded by dead bodies, seeing the violence that man had inflicted on the natural world: All the trees were blasted; all the leaves were knocked down, the ground churned to a vicious, sucking mud.

Letter after letter, poem after poem, records disgust and horror at what man has done to the landscape as well as to his own kind. You find no talk of honor or glory at all. It's man talking about the violence that man has done to man. The wheel has come full circle. Men do heroic things. Soldiers bring in their comrades under fire, but it is not seen through anything like Homer's lens of heroic action in the Trojan War.

The Enemy

Most of the poets in World War I—Rosenberg, Owen, Sorley, Sassoon—were foot soldiers, and they wrote about other foot soldiers. And they tell it how it is, illustrating the horrors of modern mechanized warfare. In the First World War, you get the sense of identity between the soldiers on both sides most movingly exemplified in the famous Christmas truce where the soldiers—not the generals—said to themselves, "Enough is enough." They sang hymns, and they came out of their trenches, and they met, and they smoked cigarettes and talked together. This was much disapproved of by the general staff.

Wilfred Owen, in his favorite poem, "Strange Meeting," has the very piercing line, "I am the enemy you killed, my friend." *Enemy* and *friend* in the same line. And David Jones who many years later wrote a truly wonderful book called *In Parenthesis*, about his experience as a foot soldier in The Great War, dedicates his poem to a whole list of Welshmen and then to "the bearded infantry with whom we exchanged loaves at a trench's intersection." All his comrades were killed on the first of July 1916, and he dedicated his account to the enemy front fighters, "against whom we found ourselves by misadventure." And so there is this strong sense of comradeship that contrasts strikingly with the clear feelings of hostility that many of the poets have.

The strong sense of companionship discernible in the poems—the letters, the diaries of all the First World War soldiers—is greatly at variance with the strong negative feelings that many of them have for the politicians, for the generals, and, much more, for the profiteers. In the poems of Owen and Sassoon particularly, this gets simplified as a conflict between the young and the old: the young men who are being needlessly sacrificed, as they see it, by the old men.

Bearing Witness through Poetry

Owen and Sassoon's vision of the poet as witness is really the root of the matter. In a sense, Homer is testifying, is bearing witness to what happens on the battlefield between the Greeks and the Trojans. Had he not written about those battles, we wouldn't know about them. And of course in the world in which we now live, there are all sorts of other ways in which successive generations will know about these wars. Photographers, radio and television reporters, print journalists are all testifying now.

But poets have a special role. In our lives, many of our emotions are rather complicated. We say we love someone, but at the same time we're a bit resentful of the fact that they do this or they said that. A good poet will get into the poem both the affection and the resentment. A really good poet gives you tremendous compression. I think the poet's armor-piercing shell has a more lasting effect than the journalist's piece written rapidly to be published in the next day's newspaper. The poet's shell also has more impact than the cool analysis of a historian writing years and years after the event he's describing. What the poets can give you is the sense of being there, and this is why I feel sometimes quite strongly that that is what poets should be doing. They should be bearing witness to what is happening in a war, in a hospital, wherever. Poets bear witness every hour of the day in all sorts of different circumstances, but I don't think that reading a newspaper is enough to justify one to bear witness against the war in Iraq.

Robert Lowell wrote a wonderful poem called "Fall 1961," in which he speaks of a father as being no shield for his child. He wrote about this as the Russian barges with their missiles were approaching Cuba, and he wondered whether the American president was going to press the button. Is World War III about to start? Lowell was telling the truth about how he felt as an American father unable to shield his child against this coming fury, if it was to come. Now that seems to me a valid and very good subject for a poet in, say, America, better than if he had written about imagining himself in the waters of Vietnam or wherever. This is particularly true in Lowell's case because he was a conscientious objector.

The Soldier-Poet Changes

In the First or the Second World Wars, a great many people who think of themselves as poets were involved in the fighting, and so naturally they write poems about the fighting. Yet in the Vietnam War, there were relatively few soldiers who thought of themselves as poets. What comes through many of the veteran poems from the Vietnam War are tremendous intensity of feeling, some very sharp perceptions, a great many very strong, jagged, visual, or aural images, but not a great deal of structural ability: the ability to put together a large body of language to achieve a single persuasive effect.

During the Vietnam War, there was a very strong body of stateside poets who became famous and went 'round to campuses reading and protesting against the war. Their poems can be broadly divided into two categories: those who wrote as Allen Ginsberg did about the effect the war was having on America and those who chose to present themselves as if they were participants, even though all they had done was read the newspapers or watch television; their poems seem to me less honorable, and certainly less good.

One thing that interests me particularly about the Vietnam War is the way in which a significant number of poets who served in the war have come to feel that it was, at least in some way, wrong, and have chosen to go back to Vietnam to meet their Vietnamese counterparts. A lot more American poets have gone back to Vietnam after the war to tell the truth, to talk to people, to be civilized, to be humane, than in the earlier wars.

It seems now that the poets have developed a sort of enlarged conscience, as if they are now more motivated by humanitarian instincts and are more likely to take a humanitarian stance. You go back to the villages that you fought over, where you killed the men, women, and children, to make some form of reparation. I find it very moving that so many poets have done this.

What poets have to do is write the best poems of which they are capable, and they normally do that by coming to grips with their subject. Not many people write very good love poems who haven't actually been in love, and not very many people write good war poems who haven't had some experience with war. Tennyson's "Charge of the Light Brigade" is an exception. In that poem, Tennyson is doing what I said poets should be very cautious about doing—writing from a newspaper report. But if you're as good a poet as Tennyson, you can get away with it.

The Times newspaper carried a piece by a famous war correspondent who was on the Heights at Balaklava and reported this extraordinary scene: On the Heights were not only the journalists but a great many ladies in their crinolines, who went out to observe the war as a sort of spectacle. They were watching on the Heights as the messages were transmitted from one horseman riding to Cardigan and Raglan. Suddenly, to everyone's astonishment, the light brigade lined up, and charged some Russian gunners. It was a terrible mistake. There was a whole battery of Russian gunners who shelled them with heavy artillery. Whoever was leading the charge knew it was a mistake. He got an order and he obeyed it.

Tennyson read Russell's report. The report spoke of the incredible heroism of these soldiers, charging the gunners. The officer in charge didn't carry a sword, because that would be rather vulgar. He just led them. The men carried the swords. He just rode. The courage was just extraordinary, but the blunder was also extraordinary, and Tennyson's poem captures the futility, the blunder, the waste. It didn't have to happen. They didn't have to do this. There would have been other ways of leaving the gunners alone, or of taking them from the side, or something.

Tennyson's poem very beautifully and sensitively conveys the exhilaration which the watchers and, I daresay some of the participants, felt in this, taking part in this extraordinary madcap heroic exploit, even as they are fully aware of the mistake.

The Eye Under the Duckboard

I don't think poets are uniquely suited to writing about war. Of course there have been wonderful novels, documentaries, even plays. R. C. Sherriff's play, *Journey's End*, is now playing in London. It is a searing and brilliant account of what it was like to be living in a forward trench in The Great War. Literature generally has been a huge educator. There's no doubt at all that for most of my generation and maybe the next generation, what they know about The Great War is much more derived from the writers than from the historians, or the filmmakers, or the novelists.

They might have read *All Quiet on the Western Front*; they might have seen the film; but they've all read Owen and Sassoon at school and they've read Robert Graves's memoirs *Goodbye to All That*, and Sassoon's memoirs. Writers have had a considerable educational impact in British society. Because poetry is a very distilled form of writing, Randall Jarrell can write a poem like "The Death of the Ball Turret Gunner," where he captures a whole life in about five lines:

"From my mother's sleep I fell into the State,
And I hunched in its belly till my wet fur froze.
Six miles from earth, loosed from its dream of life,
I woke to black flak and the nightmare fighters.
When I died they washed me out of the turret with a hose."

The image of the unborn child, or the newly born child, runs through the poem. As Jarrell explained in a note about this poem, the ball turret on a B-29 was a Plexiglas sphere set into the belly of the airplane, and it had, I think, twin machine guns. When the bomber was attacked from behind or underneath, the ball turret gunner could swivel his turret and engage the enemy. The gunner had to be small because it was a very small Plexiglas sphere. The gunner hunched in this round sphere is like a fetus in the womb. Much of the power of the poem seems to me to derive from the submerged, buried, but clearly present image of an abortion: 'When I died they washed me out of the turret with a hose.' The child doesn't wake to life. He wakes to black flak and the nightmare fighters.

And Jarrell's note says that the hose would have been a steam hose with tremendous pressure of boiling water. The idea of this poor dismembered gunner in his Plexiglas sphere being washed out with a hose has a horrible resonance with the action of an abortion. The poem is about an unnatural death. This child should have grown up and lived its life in fields, and cities, had a job, married, and had children, and all that. Instead he's dead and washed out of the turret with a hose.

That poem is very swift and very sharp, and it goes through all our armor. It hits us in the solar plexus, and we can't ever forget it. Maybe we can't remember it word-perfect, but I think one remembers that poem after one has forgotten many book-length accounts of warfare. I think much of the impact that poetry has is like an armor-piercing shell. Unlike an ordinary shell, which just explodes, an armor-piercing shell goes right through everything to reach its target, and a really good poem has that sort of sharpness and projectile force. It goes right into the imagination of the reader, who says, "Wow!"

As moved as I have been by Sassoon's *Sherston's Progress* trilogy and Edmund Blunden's *Undertones of War*, I couldn't give you a very full account of them. There's a moment in Blunden of the poet as memoirist, where he is going along his trench and a young lance corporal is making tea; the poet wishes him a good tea and then goes around the corner. Then there's a dull thud and a shell has landed, and someone's started shouting. So he goes back again and the lance corporal isn't there; there's only a black mess on the parapet. Under the duckboard there's an eye. When the eye of the reader meets the eye of the soldier under the duckboard that's something you don't forget.

Thomas Hardy *was born in Dorchester in the United Kingdom in 1840 and died in 1928, and is generally regarded as one of the greatest writers in English literature. His poem "Drummer Hodge" is about a British soldier who has gone to South Africa to fight in the Boer War of 1899-1902 and then is killed and buried there.*

Drummer Hodge

Thomas Hardy

They throw in Drummer Hodge, to rest
Uncoffined? just as found:
His landmark is a kopje-crest
That breaks the veldt around:
And foreign constellations west
Each night above his mound.

Young Hodge the drummer never knew?
Fresh from his Wessex home?
The meaning of the broad Karoo,
The Bush, the dusty loam,
And why uprose to nightly view
Strange stars amid the gloom.

Yet portion of that unknown plain
Will Hodge for ever be;
His homely Northern breast and brain
Grow to some Southern tree,
And strange-eyed constellations reign
His stars eternally.

Jonathan Schell is a peace and disarmament correspondent for the magazine The Nation, *and the author of* The Unconquerable World: Power, Nonviolence, and the Will of the People *and* The Fate of the Earth. *The following narrative was adapted from Schell's interview with Rick King for the film* Voices in Wartime.

Toward a Future Without War

Jonathan Schell

War is always a shock the first time you see it. Certainly that was true for me because I'd been living in Japan for a year and a half, and I stopped in Saigon without really having any plan or intention to be there. I was quite ignorant of what was going on in the war, because I'd been pretty well cut off from the news in Japan. It became apparent to me immediately, even though I had no general view of the war, that it wasn't making sense in its own terms. The hope was to win over the hearts and minds of the people. But if you destroy their villages, this very clearly wasn't going to serve the purpose of the war. I think the very experience of being there, of seeing it, of witnessing it, is different if you find that you can't believe in the purpose of it.

We were taken off to an airstrip early one morning and then flown for a short hop, about 15 minutes, to another airstrip in the jungle without being told what we were going to be witnessing. It turned out to be the largest military operation of the war up to that time, and in fact, subsequently, as well, because it was such a failure they didn't want to repeat the experience

We found ourselves in a dusty field talking to a captain who had a slate, on an easel. The slate was sort of like the specials at a restaurant, except that here were six or seven elements of the operation, and the reporters were permitted to go on any of those missions they chose. I chose to accompany an attack by 48 helicopters on a village that had always been run by the National Liberation Front. I asked the captain in the field what was going to happen to the people there and he said, "We ship them out." And I said, "What will you do to the village?" And he said, "Well, we're going to destroy it."

I resolved at that moment that I would follow the progress of that entire operation from its very beginning to its very end. I was plunged into the middle of that military operation with no knowledge in advance of what the war was about, with no opinion about it, so in a certain sense it was an unalloyed experience of war itself, without preparation.

The experience at Ben Suc had a decisive effect on the rest of my life, certainly. This is true, in part, for anybody who sees war for the first time. In your ordinary life back at home, you see all the apparatus of civilization. The buses, the cars, the buildings, and so forth are devoted to purposes that make sense, that seem broadly beneficial. Suddenly you see all of that turned on its head, all turned to destroying human life rather than preserving it. That's an immense and tremendous shock and in modern war especially so. In Vietnam, the disproportion between the power of the United States, with all its money and machinery and wealth and destructive power, and this very primitive and simple and poor society, presented a profoundly shocking picture to anybody witnessing it.

New Ways of Waging War

There's been a transformation of warfare that we haven't quite caught up with. Nuclear weapons have a paralyzing effect. That was certainly true during the Cold War and it remains true. You simply cannot have a world war of the kind that you had twice in the 20th century. You will not have a victory of one side and a defeat of another; you will have the annihilation of both. Warfare at that level is simply unfightable.

A new way of exerting power and settling disputes has arisen in the world. Local peoples have resolved to take charge of their own destinies. And they have invented ways of doing that that have proved highly effective in actually defeating and expelling all of the empires of the 20th century.

One of these methods was people's war, which really relied primarily on the political resolve of the local population and secondarily on military force. Military force was surely involved, and people's war is a very bloody business. But what the leaders and inventors of people's war, such as Mao Zedong and Ho Chi Minh, said with the greatest clarity is that politics must be in command. If they can't win the allegiance of local people, their military operations are going to be an absolute failure.

But other movements experimented with and found ways of opposing occupations without any violence whatsoever. The most dramatic example is Gandhi's nonviolent movement against the British in India, which was successful in defeating the greatest empire of its time. The others were the movements, beginning in Eastern Europe and then spreading into Russia, against the Soviet empire, with all its resources of violence, from nuclear weapons to the KGB to the Red Army. Highly effective means of defeating superior force have been discovered, and they've remade the map of the Earth in the 20th century as much as violence has.

Throughout most of history, war has, in fact, been what people have said it is: namely the *ultima ratio*, or the final arbiter. It's been the means of deciding things that could not be otherwise decided, and that is written throughout all the centuries of history. It really hasn't been until modern times that other means have arisen.

Paralysis and People's War

The paralysis imposed by nuclear weapons reached quite far down into the system, dampening even conventional wars. Among nonnuclear powers, especially in the Cold War, the danger was very present that a conventional war would lead to a nuclear war, which would drag in the nuclear powers. In response to this paralysis, and taking advantage of it, was the rise of people's war.

Conventional war depended on the idea that the person with superior forces was going to be the winner—until it became paralyzed and there could no longer be winners or losers. People's war depended entirely on something else, and that was the political allegiance of ordinary people in local situations within countries. The power exerted there was of a fundamentally different kind, even though it would often result in the use of force. It ultimately was a kind of political power depending on this allegiance. That's why, very typically in a people's war, the end would come when the opposing army would throw down its arms and defect, as an exhibit of political power. This change in will, hearts, and minds was decisive. So, in this situation of paralyzed conventional war, paralyzed by nuclear weapons, people's war arose as a means of fighting that was still possible and highly successful

Vietnam is the ideal example of a people's war. There you had a nuclear-armed superpower with virtually endless military resources that was actually defeated by a very poor, small country without that much weaponry at its disposal. And the reason is a very simple one: They won the political war in their own country, and there was nothing that the United States could do to reverse that. It could occupy Vietnam forever and fight there forever, but it couldn't set up a government that would be popular with its own people and also friendly to the United States. So it turned out that in the contest between military force and the political power exhibited in people's war, the people's war was eventually the winner: Political power eventually trumped military power.

America, right now, however, is rejecting the lesson of Vietnam. It's rejecting the lesson of the anticolonial movements of the 20th century. We are acting as if we can still impose our will through our tremendously superior military forces. While it's true that you can win all the military battles, I don't think ultimately you can win that way, because you can't win the political battle. And at the end of the day, it's the political battle that's decisive

The experience of the soldiers in Vietnam is very relevant to the experience of the soldiers in Iraq, because in Vietnam, the soldiers had the experience of fighting a war for a people that wanted them to leave. In short, they faced people's war, and in people's war, it's not just the soldiers of the other side who hate you and are fighting you; it's the population as a whole.

And immediately American soldiers felt this; they knew they were hated in the villages that they went into. And they were hated not only by the Viet-Cong or the NLF; they were hated by ordinary people: old women, old men, children, who indeed would be giving support to the NLF. So the dreadful temptation, the dreadful mistake, which is almost inevitable in that situation, is that you start making war against the people. After all, the people are making war against you. You start to shoot the old women; you start to burn the villages; you start to bomb and destroy the villages.

No matter how many battles you win, you continue to lose the war, because it all depends on politics and what the people think. It's the most frustrating, most brutalizing kind of warfare, and it looks as if we've headed into the same kind of situation in Iraq. In both cases [Vietnam and Iraq], what they are facing is resistance by the local population. The irony is that they believe they're there to help the local people, but it turns out that the local people do not want help. They do not appreciate it, and they support the resistance to the American occupation.

War Poetry Today

Poetry traditionally has addressed war in two ways. The first is the glamour of warfare, "The Charge of the Light Brigade," the heroism of warfare, celebrating war, celebrating the cause, the sacrifice, and so on. The other, of course, is the horror of war, such as Wilfred Owen's poems about the First World War.

The greatest poems can encompass both. *The Iliad* does that, and there's a wonderful essay by the French philosopher Simone Weil called *The Iliad*, or the *Poem of Force* in which she describes the poem in exactly this light. Obviously, war is still with us in both of those senses in various forms. But now it's got a new aspect: the element of mass-destruction, more specifically, the danger that our species will blow itself off the face of the earth with these weapons. Since 1945, that has been the fundamental human question posed by nuclear war, if you want to call a nuclear war a war at all.

The problem is that the end of the world is nothing. What is there to write about? How do you come to grips with it? I've looked and there really isn't very much outstanding poetry that addresses this problem. They come up against this central problem of nothingness. How do you describe that? That's a new riddle for poetry, just as it's a new riddle for all of us. If poetry is about war, if poetry is about love, if poetry is about time, then all of these are eclipsed, taken off the table, in the extinction of our species. In Shakespeare's sonnet, he's constantly saying to his beloved, "Your beauty is fading, but it will be preserved in my lines." This is a theme of poetry. But if nobody is there to read the poems, then the beauty is not preserved.

Robert Lowell is one of the few poets who has addressed war and the end of the world, at least in one poem, "Fall 1961." He talks about "all autumn, the chafe and jar of nuclear war." Those words, *chafe* and *jar*, which are surprising words, resonate with nuclear danger in a way that I'm powerless to explain. Maybe it's something to do with the abrasion of living through that time, which is, of course, the Cuban Missile Crisis. But he also says, "We talked our extinction to death," which is a very nice, very powerful line. Somehow it helps to capture the futility of the whole business.

We Need a New Way

Looking back on it, I would say that violence has become utterly self-defeating, as manifested and symbolized by the fact that we actually threaten to wipe ourselves off the face of the earth with it. It is bankrupt; it is no way to go, if it ever was one. Whatever utility or virtues it may once have had have been utterly lost, and so we need a new way of doing things. We need to find another way of conducting our business, another way of fighting, if you will.

The wonderful thing, and the most important thing about what I seek to offer here, is that such a way has been found. In human affairs, a kind of political power, not military power, is acting that can actually overmatch and defeat violence and has repeatedly done so. It's not a magic thing, it's not a panacea—it involves suffering and struggle. It sometimes succeeds, it sometimes fails, but it is a way to go. It's something to try; it's something to develop at this impasse with respect to violence.

We should turn away from violence. We should start to turn away from it comprehensively and start turning toward these other ways of doing things. And these other ways are not only a matter of direct action, but also, from my point of view, of democratic government: the liberties, the rights, the checks and balances. Democratic government is an institutional expression of the same kind of power that arises when people agree with one another on common purposes and resolve to act together to conduct their affairs in a lawful manner; without torture in the basement, without gunfire at the local television station, without a *coup d'etat* to bring the next regime into power.

I'm very pacifistic, but I'm not a pacifist. I can conceive of situations in which the use of force is necessary, or where I would accept it, or advocate it, or do it myself even. In situations of crimes against humanity, genocide, for example, it could be necessary for the international community to step in very quickly and stop it with force. Whether we could ever arrive at a world where force would be removed entirely from the picture, well, I wouldn't know. That's not my point: My point is that we need a sea change. We need to place our faith, our effort, our inventive energy into these other kinds of action that are more promising, that are more fruitful, that steadily draw down the reliance on force and build up our reliance on these other means.

In practical terms, you have to do things slowly, carefully, and gradually. You have to invite other countries to step into the gap. The United States should step back militarily. Then maybe some other countries would build up a little bit in order to create the possibility of truly international action and intervention when that is required.

Making the enormous expenditures we do on military dominance is an absolute waste of effort. Our reliance on military power as the mainstay of American policy is a profound mistake. We impoverish ourselves. And by "impoverish" I don't mean only economic impoverishment; we forgo the tremendous opportunities that we have to act in other cooperative, helpful ways: with aid, with assistance, in concert with allies in other countries. Instead, we seem to be relying almost entirely on military force. It's 180 degrees in the wrong direction.

Part 4:
BEYOND WARTIME

John Henry Parker is a veteran of the Marine Corps and
executive director of Veterans and Families. His father was a combat
veteran from the Korean War, and his son returned home in 2004 after
serving in the U.S. Army in Afghanistan. This narrative is adapted from
Parker's interview with Andrew Himes for the short documentary film
Beyond Wartime.

Let's Get It Right This Time

John Henry Parker

My son is a sergeant in the 10th Mountain Division. He was in
Afghanistan for the second time, and I hadn't heard from him
very much at all. One day he called me from the Pakistan border. I
could kind of sense that there was something really going on with
him. He started explaining to me that he had some real concerns
about coming home and being able to connect with his children
and his wife; he was really concerned to the point where he just
declared that he was going to need some serious counseling when
he came home. It was just really alarming as a parent to hear this
from your son, and it was really emotional and very difficult to deal
with at the time.

He was a squad leader, and his job was to go into the border
towns and into the different mountain areas around the Pakistan
border to seek out and find the enemy. The Taliban, al Qaeda, and
whoever else might be hiding in the hills resisting. He had been
witnessing a lot of really horrific things, and his main concern was,
"Can I come back and just get past all this and be a dad, a husband,
and just be a family guy. How do you do that?"

What it conjures up for me is memories of my own upbringing,
with my dad, who was a combat veteran from Korea. All I know
about my father's experience is that he was in the Marine Corps, and
he was in Korea. He didn't talk about it and he won't talk about it.
Recently I did talk to him about his experience. He said that he went

to go seek help initially, but the therapists seemed like they were more concerned with things that were important to them; they didn't really relate to him, so he immediately went into shutdown mode and never went back. Consequently, I was raised around a guy who I knew loved me, but who was very volatile, very scary. It was terrorizing. He didn't even realize how he was affecting us as children. He was always very angry, very volatile.

My son was talking to me about his concerns about coming home—he has two beautiful little kids—and his worries about transitioning back. I immediately went into panic mode. I felt a lot of anxiety about knowing I had to do something. I thought it would be simple, I thought it would be more straightforward, that there would be resources more readily available. Having been in the Marine Corps myself, and transitioning back into civilian life, I realized that there's not a lot of care about bringing these guys back. I was optimistic but I was also concerned, so I started doing a lot of research to figure out what he needed when he came home and how could I find him some resources. I spent the next few months in a very frustrated place.

Back in Vietnam, when they would send these guys back, they called it "Foxhole to front porch." Literally in a very short amount of time they went from one place to another. The circumstances in which my son came home were very similar. He returned in an emergency leave situation, so, literally, within 72 hours of leaving Afghanistan, he was back in his house. He called me and he said, "You know, just a few days ago I was in Afghanistan literally being shot at and in firefights, and in a really high-stress environment. And now I'm cooking eggs for my kids." He was just trying to get his head around that.

Helping PTSD Sufferers: What to Do and Not Do

In today's military, they're really trying to take them through a critical incident debriefing and a process of decompression as much as they can, so it's not typical for it to be that quick. He was joking about it but it was interesting to hear him say, "I haven't been touched by another person in nine months. I have been with my buddies, and we've been in really extreme situations, and to come home . . . " it was funny, he said, "you know, my wife's like a spider monkey. She just wants to be with me and all around me, and I get to the point where I just can't handle it, and then she misunderstands. So it's been a real adjustment trying to figure out how to come back and rejoin my family."

What's been explained to me by my son is that what keeps you alive is hope, and you know, thinking about your parents or your significant other or your girlfriend. You want to get home. There is an interesting process where the person comes home, and they're used to being around a certain set of people in a very intense environment. Then family members, in a very well intentioned way, have a bunch of big parties and get-togethers, and that can be the wrong thing to do, having too many people too quickly approaching this person and asking him how was it over there. Just the fact of being around a lot of people is very challenging for guys who come home. We had a get-together at our place, but before we had it, I had an agreement with my son that if he got uncomfortable, he could just go out and have a cigarette, go out to the truck, and I'd take care of it with everybody. It wouldn't be any big deal. I would say two-thirds of the time, he was out at the truck; he wasn't interacting with anyone.

A lot of the military people I talk to really appreciate people saying thank you, and they just really want what they've been through over there to mean something, especially if they lost buddies and other people they care about. I think that's what's most important. My son Danny told me that even walking through the airport talking to friends, he always feels the wheels turning in their heads. There are really two questions that people consistently ask that set him off in the wrong direction, which are: "How was it over there?" and "How many of those fill-in-the-blank did you kill?" I think that is really insensitive, and people don't even realize it. It forces him to constantly have to tell a little story just to shut them up and get rid of them, and move on to some other topic. He's amazed but literally 80-90 percent of the people just want to know the answers to those two questions. I think that it would be better if people really understood that just by asking the question, you're really asking them to re-experience something that could be extremely stressful for them. That's not really a good place to delve into with a veteran.

The single most important thing about my son's healing process is really talking about his experiences, and getting it out—not holding it in and not compartmentalizing it. The statistics from the military's own research say that upwards of 17 percent of our guys coming back from Iraq are suffering from post-traumatic stress disorder. The *Los Angeles Times* quoted a statistic of 23 percent. What's interesting is that we've got these statistics, but upwards of 60 percent of the people who need help the most won't seek help, for myriad reasons. That's really the biggest challenge, this high-risk group of people. We, as a community, really need to focus on them.

You know we, in the military, have lived a code, of an Army of One, the few the proud the Marines, adapt overcome improvise. There's nothing in there that says: Seek help. Clearly, 75 percent of the guys coming back are going to need to adjust to civilian life and become very productive. Some of the great leaders of business historically have been former military. It is really evident that the majority of people coming back are going to be very productive in civilian life. It's the at-risk population that we really need to focus on. It's never been done before.

Building Support Networks

When I talk with people about Veterans and Families, and how we're trying to build a support network of family members, employers, and community leaders, the overwhelming response I get is: "Let's get it right this time. Let's learn from the past." It's really refreshing. Literally, every person I talk to, whether it's a teenager or a young adult or a baby boomer, have all had an experience of being raised in a home with a Vietnam veteran father or grandfather or mother, or they've had some experience of what happened. The young people know that something terrible happened with this homecoming, and the people who experienced it never want to see it happen to their kids. So the message of "let's get homecoming right this time" is really the message that we're trying to put out to the community about building the support network.

To my son Danny I would say, "This is a long-term process, and it's going to take time. You've got incredible family support around you, everyone believes in you, and we're here for you. We're going to make a difference for all of your buddies coming back who maybe aren't seeking help, as you are. We're going to make a difference in the community, and you're a part of that. Your message and ability to talk to other people and allow me to talk about your experiences are going to touch a lot of people and it's going to make a big difference in their lives, for both the veterans and the people who are trying to understand what is going on for this person coming home. It also shows communities how they can be appropriate in managing their emotions and their patience and their understanding about how to let this person readjust, maybe little by little, and allow them to open up."

I can say that looking at my experience in healing and the research that's available to us, and talking to countless veterans and family members, the 60 percent of the PTSD sufferers who aren't going to seek counseling are going to feel like somehow they're failing, or they're going to be stigmatized. So we, as a society, need to understand that this is what's happening, and need to create opportunities for personal development, for programs that are more private, individualized, and self-paced for veterans. My experience is that veterans across the board are very interested in succeeding and being effective, but it's not always counseling that's going to help them. It's about reading a book, going to a seminar, going to a self-paced learning program. What that does is open a possibility for thinking about who you're becoming as a person, rather than where you've been.

I remember when I got out of the Marine Corps, the best advice I received from a military officer was: "You're going to get out of the military and it's going to be a lot different than you remember. My advice is to go to a bookstore, go to the self-help section, and find a book that jumps off the shelf at you. Start reading it, and focus on who you're becoming." I think that my advice to any serviceperson, is: Don't close down; find a hobby, find a book, go to a seminar, find a program, find something so you can start individually expressing to yourself who you want to be. Develop a new identity. That military experience, that armor and that responsiveness will always be there, and you'll be able to recapture it in a second. But you may not need to go there ever again in your life. I would say focus on a learning path.

I have this memorial bracelet, and it symbolizes the three guys who were lost in my son's unit when they were in Afghanistan. I wear it every day as a reminder of why I'm doing what I'm doing as a parent, and why I'm building this community support network. So it means a lot.

Dr. Enas Mohamed, an Iraqi physician, is on the board of the Iraq Community Center in Seattle, Washington. Dr. Mohamed toured Baghdad hospitals and neighborhoods in November of 2004 in order to sum up the medical needs of the Iraqi civilian population. Dr. Mohamed is a researcher into effects of depleted uranium on cancers and other diseases at a research center in Seattle. The following narrative was adapted from her interview with Andrew Himes for the film Beyond Wartime.

The Need for Hope: Civilian Casualties of War

Dr. Enas Mohamed

~

I left Iraq on September 7, 1997, at age 34. I had lived most of my adult life as a doctor in Iraq. The Iran-Iraq War lasted for eight years, from 1981 to 1988, which were the eight years that I was in medical school. The first year I entered medical school, I couldn't have imagined that I would graduate and the war would still be going on. The Iran-Iraq War didn't have a direct impact on the major cities; its effects were mainly on the Iraq-Iran border, mostly in the suburban areas of Basra in southern Iraq.

The sense of the Gulf War was totally different. The main target was Baghdad, as well as other major cities. We experienced a kind of horror. I can't really forget it. I was hoping that one day I could, but I can't—the first day especially, when suddenly we woke up because of the siren. It was about 5 a.m. on January 17, 1991. You don't imagine when you sleep, after you've said goodnight to your family, that you will be being bombed awake. We were prepared, but we didn't know when zero hour for this war would be. There were still negotiations between the governments. Once the siren started going, everybody was riveted with horror. All you could hear was bombs falling one after the other, one after the other, from different directions.

The kids were really scared, and kept yelling. At that time, I was with my family, and suddenly the power went out. It was winter, and so, at 5 a.m. there was not much sunlight, it was dark, and the bombing continued. Everybody felt a deep fear in their bones. We decided at that time that we should leave. We had never imagined it was going to be a real war. Then a lot of window glass started smashing, and there was the sound of everybody running, looking for their kids, who had started running, looking for a place to get away, to hide somewhere to be away from the glass. That's when we realized, yes, it's going to be a real, real war.

We ran away to another suburban area, north of Baghdad, but it continued for 42 days. During these 42 days, there was heavy, heavy bombing on Iraq and no power. When I say, "No power," I mean, no traffic lights—more car accidents, more victims. No power means no hospitals. A few hospitals only, the main medical centers in Baghdad, had backup generators to work. No power means no factories, people can't go to work anymore, which means increased unemployment, more poverty, more malnutrition. No power means no school— there's no light, no heat, no visual aids, but students didn't give up. Yes, attendance was at a very low rate, but we continued teaching after the cease fire. When you say "no power" it is not a simple phrase, it means the whole city is paralyzed. Just like when people here live without power for even a few hours . . . I remember the black out last year, in New York.

In the fall of 2004, I went to Baghdad, and I visited a lot of hospitals. Among them was Al-Yarmouk hospital, which is one of the main medical centers in Baghdad. I witnessed a lot of casualties from one of the car bombings that happened the day before, which unfortunately happened just a few hours after my arrival in Baghdad. I was really astonished when I saw the cases. The only things that could be done were rudimentary first-aid measures. They didn't really get enough medical care. First of all, there was no x-ray machine, and you can imagine, the injuries from these types of terrorist attacks would be mainly broken bones. So they were trying to guess what kind of broken bones they had and treat accordingly. Thank God there were so many efficient doctors who were still there, because I've heard about so many of them who have left the country because of the kidnapping and the stealing issues.

These casualties were not just adults. I felt so sorry for the many kids, who were among the casualties because it happened in a very populated area, and in daytime. It was at 10 in the morning. The hospital was really suffering from a deficiency of so many supplies, and the number of doctors was diminished by close to 50 percent from the days when I was there. I used to work in this hospital and I know usually how many doctors are supposed to be in each ward. I can't blame them. So many doctors just left the country because of the hard conditions; they couldn't even secure their families.

The Devastating Effects of Depleted Uranium

Another major issue facing the Iraqi people is the problem of depleted uranium. Depleted uranium is a waste product from enriched uranium that is highly radioactive. Each ton of enriched uranium would produce four tons of depleted uranium, when they use it in a nuclear reactor. To get rid of such high-risk radioactive material, they invented a new way to use it in armor. If they cover a bullet with depleted uranium, it will enable this bullet to go through a thick wall. In addition to the bullets coated with that layer of depleted uranium, the tanks are covered with a shell of it because it makes it very hard for any missile to destroy the tank.

During the war there will be a lot of munitions, and they may need tons of depleted uranium to hit a few targets. So, tons of these missiles might be dumped on the ground and stay there. The problem with the depleted uranium is that it has a radiation effect that may last for 4.5 billion years. So although they say that it has a very low effect due to the alpha particles, if you are exposed over many years, this effect will be cumulative in your body; it will enhance mutations, and motivate the chromosomes to create abnormal cells, most probably cancer cells.

Besides the effect of the ion itself, the problem with these alpha particles as reproduced by these depleted uranium particles is that it has a great affinity for bonding to the liver, kidney, and brain; it can stay forever, in the lungs, also. The only way for these particles to enter the body is through inhalation or ingestion. So it will enter the body and start working from there, with time. Iraqis will be exposed to this toxic material as long as they are living in Iraq.

In general, there is some research but we can't prove it yet, that this is the cause of all the weird kinds of tumors that we are suffering from in Iraq. I've witnessed many cases myself. We have high rates of birth defects, high rates of miscarriages, like we never had before; many children who have leukemia. I found a girl who is 11 years old who has ovarian cancer. This is so weird; usually we have this kind of cancer late in life. These people have been exposed to this kind of radiation since the first Gulf War, when they first started using this kind of ammunition in the world. Nobody had tested it before. Besides the Iraqi citizens, the American soldiers themselves are suffering now from the effects of using depleted uranium in the ammunition. This problem will last forever if we don't stop it.

Children are usually the most vulnerable victims in any war. They don't have that much strength, starting with their physical strength and their immune system, so they will get infections more easily than adults. There are not many antibiotics available, or even the supportive measures that we need, such as IV fluids. You had to get it from the black market.

Injured or Infected Children: The Long-term Effects

You can't imagine the amount of disease that has spread since the war. One of the largest issues is polluted water: It causes dysentery, cholera, typhoid, and there is a deficiency of water, so we don't have enough water to wash our hands every time they get dirty. We try to save it for when there's a critical need to wash your hands. Children play together all the time, and they don't take precautions like adults do. Plus, they have weaker immune systems and malnutrition—or not enough of the right food to fulfill their needs as growing kids. With the low level of hygiene and the high level of malnutrition, any infection will start to grow and transmit very quickly. We have deficiencies even in vaccines (we still suffer from TB), so a newborn without vaccines will be exposed to these bacteria from the very first days of his life.

One of the victims was a very very hard case for me. He was like, 10 or 11 years old. I talked to his mom, and learned his history: He left school to support his family, so he was on his way to sell some cigarettes near the street where a car bomb exploded. This little child got broken hands and broken legs; the doctor told me that they might have to amputate one of his legs. And I can't imagine what that means for a 10-year-old boy—to live with one limb. He didn't even get enough time to finish his schooling, to play soccer, to do all activities like a little boy would do. And one of his hands also needed to be operated on. If he had gotten enough medical help at the right time, he would survive. But the problem is that there's a long waiting list for the operation, so he had to wait.

If we think about the future of such a boy, five years from now, what kind of destiny may he face. I think if the situation continued the way I saw it, this boy could hardly survive, because he would be living on the streets, selling cigarettes that wouldn't even help him to get enough income. Then, if he stopped going to school because of the poverty level, there will no future for him, no education, no degree. So he will continue living in this low income and his disability, which means he has little chance of getting a good job or training for a real job in Iraq, with our limited facilities. It would be hard for him to survive.

If we think about an orphaned girl, who is 15 years old, what kind of future might she have. It's hard for boys these days to have enough courage to go to school, so, what about the girls? Unfortunately, such a girl might go for the easiest way—prostitution. So many girls might also choose a more decent way to work, such as being a servant or taking some low-income job; it depends on her luck, if she gets a good family who will help support her . . . It's so hard for girls, for teenagers, or even a kid, 11 or 12, to find a good future in the situation that is happening now in Iraq. Without school, without good financial support, without parents to give them shelter and enough food to survive, they might die, an infectious disease might kill them, a tumor, from depleted uranium, a bomb in any street that they may walk by—you name it; it's a long long list of hazards.

What We Can Do

I think it's time to start to stop it and do something really positive for these innocent people. We have a lot of negative things in our lives. If we think about the new generation, starting with the boy I mentioned before, you can imagine a whole generation of disabled people. They have been punished for nothing. They are innocent civilians who were just hoping to live, like any other human on earth.

I am hoping, if we could work together to heal such a wound, for such a boy—and this was just one example among thousands in Iraq—we could help such kids get prosthetic limbs, enter rehab centers, learn the skills to later earn a real income for their families at some real job that doesn't require a lot of physical activities. We can modify some jobs for these kids in order to help them have a real future, any kids who survived the bombing.

But the problem is that we need proof. And I think it would be a very effective proof, if we offer for this kid, a good chance to survive. Otherwise, if he does survive, his hostility against Americans will be forever. He will be disabled and, in a poor family, it is so hard to operate with a disabled member. I mean, they can hardly live. How come they should support someone who is unable to provide any income? They will never be able to fulfill his demands, and at the same time, this guy will suffer forever. With this hostility, with this inability to do anything positive in his life, there will be a whole generation of people like him filled with negative energy toward the whole world. I think it's time to help, and to stop this disaster from going on forever.

I believe that Americans can do a lot with their resources. Starting with psychological support, which means a lot, believe me, even if it is not really a physical thing; it will help a lot at least to build a good humanitarian relationship. We need to tell Iraqis that Americans are really good people who feel Iraqis' pain deeply inside their hearts, and that they really want to help. We can start, for example, with good financial support for any Iraqi student who is unable to pay for his studies by establishing a financial aid system just like the very successful one that we have here. If we can manage a scholarship program for Iraqi students, we can help by teaching them good skills to get good jobs.

It's not only about sending money; it's about helpful thoughts, and it's about sharing successful experiences. I think if any American was really able to help, I can tell him exactly where he can put his efforts and what kinds of things he can participate in. By gathering some money, and putting it in the right place, like an official organization, or a teaching institution, something that is officially documented, this money will go to the right places. Unfortunately a lot of people will be taken advantage of and end up sending money to the wrong people. This is something we need to avoid, especially in this critical time. We need to put all our efforts together in order to utilize all the help that America can afford, and make it a real achievement by saying "This project was sponsored by American friends who really want to help."

Here is one idea I have found really effective: I've heard about a small village in southern Baghdad that was built by Saddam Hussein's guys. It was intended to be for widows, who lost their husbands during the Iran-Iraq War. He did it for propaganda purposes, and he didn't really build healthy houses. They were in very poor condition, and these people are without income so they can't afford to fix them. It would be so helpful if we support a project that can give this group of widows and orphans new skills. We found that if we just build one school, that's enough for everybody in this village to participate in and teach them regular classes, such as some cooking skills—anything that can help them to start to build their own businesses and get a regular income to support themselves, instead of going to the negative way, like prostitution, or stealing. So many crimes started growing in Iraq. Now you find people selling drugs in the streets, which is something that we've never experienced before in Iraq. So when you reach a very high level of poverty among a lot of people, they will start to do a lot of bad things.

Instead, we could give Iraqis a chance to have a good future, a chance to hope, which is a dream for every Iraqi nowadays.

The Nuts & Bolts of PTSD: An Insider's View

/

Sheila Sebron

Sheila Sebron is a disabled African-American Air Force veteran living with chronic post-traumatic stress disorder (PTSD) and severe pain. She was injured in a non-combat, service-related accident. Once a "throw-away soldier" in a wheelchair, she learned to walk, lost more than 80 pounds, and now teaches combat veterans and other trauma survivors how to recover, rehabilitate, and reintegrate into the community. As a published author and international trainer with more than 25 years of experience in workforce- and business-development for numerous government, private, and non-profit organizations, Sheila writes and lectures on suicide prevention and trauma recovery.

~

Diagnosed more than 20 years ago, I didn't finally understand the disorder that controlled my life for so long until just a few years ago. Most people don't even realize what it is, especially those of us diagnosed with the disorder. We hear the phrase, "post-traumatic stress disorder" but don't know the serious, potentially disabling effects it can have on the rest of our lives.

Post-traumatic stress disorder is a normal, human reaction to an abnormal amount of stress. The human mind and body are designed to withstand a certain amount of stress over a lifetime. The physiological reaction to fear and uncontrollable stress triggers the release of hormones that are designed to protect us in times of danger. The disorder comes when the "danger trigger" is overused, creating an abnormal reaction to future stress. As I understand it, our ability, post-trauma, to return to "normal" decides whether we will develop post-traumatic stress disorder or not. Faced with a situation that the body and/or mind perceives as acute danger, human survival responses automatically take over, superseding all other thoughts and behaviors. The physiological, uncontrollable response to severe stress is an unavoidable reaction hard-wired into our brains as a means of protecting the body from death. In my case, it is the physical experience of pain that my body interprets as "acute danger."

I Have PTSD

For me, having chronic, severe PTSD means losing a part of everyday life before the day even starts. I already know I can expect to spend half of every day caught in the echoes of thoughts, and intense feelings that are constant reminders of my original trauma. Although doctors have always told me that the pain won't kill me, my body's natural fight-or-flight response is the same as if I was bleeding to death or facing some other life-threatening situation. Over the years, the chronic pain caused by my physical injuries has repeatedly flooded my body with so many fight-or-flight signals triggering hormonal reactions that my mind and body no longer function normally.

The unexpected, unavoidable (and seemingly pointless) pain and associated anxiety I have experienced over the past 20 years act as a trigger, placing abnormal stress on my body's normal survival mechanism. I suffered through years of horrendous, relentless pain, inadequate or tortuous medical treatment, and little or no information about the long-term effects of this incurable disorder on my mental and physical health. I was never told about the cumulative effects of my body's normal response to such abnormal stress or the permanent impact on my brain's ability to function.

As a result of so many years of pain without adequate medical treatment (physical or mental), my mind is unable to accurately interpret the severity of pain, or decide on an appropriate, healthy response to pain. My inability to recognize and react appropriately to pain was clearly illustrated by the dental work I endured a few years ago. I went to the dentist for what I thought were two cavities that were causing some minor pain with occasional spikes of intense pain, but discovered that both teeth had rotted through the entire tooth to the nerve. The teeth were so severely damaged that one had to be pulled immediately, and the other required a root canal.

My body became my prison, subjecting me to terrifying events on a daily basis. My internal guide became worthless, making me feel worthless. I lost my ability to identify what was safe or normal. On a fundamental level, my survival instincts became something I had to ignore. I received a "life sentence" of increasingly diminished mental capacity as a companion to the tortuous pain I am told will never go away. People who suffer from severe, chronic pain know how it can utterly disrupt and damage one's life. Constant pain wears you down, turning the simplest of tasks into a choice of more intentional torture. Living with pain makes it hard to enjoy even the simplest daily activities, and certainly making it a challenge to carry out an exercise routine and other healthy activities.

I Got Treatment—and Answers

After 20 years of unsuccessful efforts to understand and stop my symptoms on my own, I finally began receiving treatment a few years ago. During treatment, I started to realize the true impact of this disorder on my life and my ability to function and make healthy decisions. Although I am now finally getting most of the medical care I need, my symptoms would have been far less severe and chronic if I had not been denied access to timely, effective treatment. As I began to understand the cause, symptoms, and long-term effects of PTSD, I started looking for ways to reduce my symptoms and regain control of my mind.

Sometimes, when I have severe back pain, I feel like I'm back in the car at the moment of impact. It only lasts part of a second, but is like I am really there. It makes my heart beat faster and my chest feel tight. Until recently, I didn't understand that I was remembering more of the moment of impact. Knowing that makes it worse, because I'm terrified of remembering everything. It must have been really bad pain for me to "check out" the way I have all these years. Sometimes, it feels like I might go crazy if I remember the moment of impact that stretched my body, causing permanent damage to my spine, and creating a permanent cycle of pain and recurrent memories of the moment that changed my life forever.

Because my pain level is *always* at least a 7 (on a scale of 1 to 10), it is difficult for me to talk about (or even think about) what happened to me in the accident without having a "flashback" to the moment of impact. I am realizing that I have always had intermittent, uncontrollable flashbacks whenever my back pain reaches a certain level. It's like I am feeling part of the impact, but as I am starting to feel the pain of the impact, I leave the memory. I have never remembered the entire accident, and I really don't want to. Although I have been having them for over 20 years, it wasn't until recently that I even understood the flashbacks. After it is over, I still feel the residual anxiety, but no current cause. It's like the past is the present for a moment. Sometimes it is hard to know which is more real.

PTSD is not to be taken lightly. It is a devastating illness that robs its victims of free will and imposes a slow death sentence that kills the human spirit. I get caught in these loops in my mind and get stuck thinking about part of a thought without being able to finish the thought. It gets harder and harder to do the simplest of things because I can't concentrate on anything long enough to finish a task. Multistep tasks are even harder and sometimes impossible, because I can't link the pieces of thoughts into an instruction that makes sense. Even if I can, I frequently forget what I'm doing because all of the pieces of thoughts get jumbled while I perform them.

Today, I continue to search for ways to "rewire" my brain so that I can make healthy decisions and live a normal life. I still struggle with written words, because of the multiple steps and mental instructions required to get the information from my brain to paper. It is clear that I will never be able to work a regular job again, but I remain confident that I will find something I can do, even if it is only a few hours a week.

Healing Is Possible

Thanks to finally getting the treatment I need for my PTSD, I can now break the cycle of being "trapped in my mind" and can communicate verbally. My personal experiences and work with others has convinced me that healing is possible, even after many years of untreated symptoms. By healing, I don't mean "good as new," as if nothing ever happened. Healing leaves us with "battle scars," but closes the gaping, open wounds of the untreated trauma. I meet many who also believe that life after severe trauma can leave us feeling more aware and alive. We are changed, yet somehow more human because of it. We can heal from the original trauma, and we can reduce the PTSD symptoms that have maintained the disabling effects of the trauma.

In my opinion, the basic components of an effective PTSD recovery program include
- A safe place (physically and emotionally) to share thoughts and feelings
- Compassionate support and encouragement
- Patience and self-acceptance as you learn about the "new you"
- Self-paced progress in absorbing painful thoughts, feelings, and memories
- Acceptance of grief and feelings of loss (fear, sadness, anger, guilt, depression)
- Frequent "time outs" to rest and restore your body to the relaxed state it needs to heal

Prevention Is Better Than Healing

War harms everyone it touches. Soldiers, civilians, refugees, family members, and friends—no one escapes without trauma. Trauma that we fail to address will only lead to continued, renewed, or fresh conflict. I didn't plan to open my life to public scrutiny, but I believe that by sharing my story, I have a chance to help prevent the potential epidemic of PTSD among my fellow soldiers currently experiencing the traumatic stress of war. Today, I am sharing my story and my fight for the legal, humane, fair, and unbiased treatment that the law promises and every American soldier deserves. By drawing attention to my case, I hope other American soldiers, especially those recovering from the effects of war, will have an opportunity to get the treatment they will need to avoid developing this permanent, and disabling, disorder.

Beverley Boos, *executive director of* Opening of the Heart, *is a photographer of essence and transformation. She photographs relationships: between people or in nature, in commercial work and architecture; and between the human spirit and social change. The following narrative was adapted from Boos' interview with Andrew Himes for the film* Beyond Wartime.

Opening of the Heart

Beverly Boos

I was in the Territories, in the West Bank, and I was doing a special series on child victims of violence, tortured children in particular. It was my last opportunity of the day; I was traveling with Children's Defense International and my Palestinian host, and they mentioned to me that there was a little girl in Doura village, which is at the edge of Hebron, who had a bullet in her head.

We went to see her. Her name was Marwa Al-Sharif. She was sitting on a bed in the shadows, with a big bandage wrapped around her head, in the sweltering heat of the summer. She actually got out of that bed and offered me cookies. Her mother showed me her x-ray, and in it you see the bullet positioned in the middle of her head. You have this little head with this three-inch copper-plated rifle round just sitting in her head. I said, "When is she having the bullet removed, what's the next step?" and they informed me that she couldn't get to a hospital that had the facilities to remove the bullet. So basically, the answer was, she's waiting for her appointment; her next check-up was in two weeks. This 10-year-old child had been in a coma for five days and then endured nightly skirmishes, conflict, tank-shelling in the distance. As I left, I thought, "I can't leave that child here, sitting with a bullet in her head and just go on about my life."

I went back to Bethlehem where numerous press people were staying. I called a press conference that day. I was going to ask if Marwa could go into Israel and have the bullet removed. I was looking for someone to take responsibility for this child who had a bullet in her head. But right at the moment our press conference was to begin, a suicide bomb went off in Jerusalem. That was a suicide bomb that took the life of another 10-year-old child, an Israeli girl, Yocheved Shushan, and of course I lost everyone; all the news teams went to the scene to perform their work.

We didn't have the press conference. It struck me that at this moment when I was calling for help for the Palestinian child with a bullet in her head, that this 10-year-old Israeli child was killed by a suicide bomb: The futility and the senselessness of this violence struck me, and of course, at the same time, I have my own 10-year-old, who was down in the Caribbean riding jet skis and living that life, and somehow the three of them formed a triangle around me and inspired me to move forward with this work.

Healing by Bearing Witness

In the case of Marwa al-Sharif, the Palestinian girl, we fortunately found a sponsor and were able to bring her to Connecticut. She came to the United States in August 2001, just before September 11, to have the bullet removed. A Connecticut hospital sponsored the operation. They told us that within one week the bullet would have migrated to her sensory systems and she would have died. I just got back from visiting her, and she's now quite the tall string-bean teenager.

I became acquainted with Yocheved Shushan's family in the hospital. The family welcomed me into their period of seven days of mourning for the 10-year-old who was lost. She had an older sister, a 15-year-old named Miriam Shushan, who survived the same suicide bombing and allowed me to photograph her in the hospital while her body was being held together with metal stays— not knowing whether she would even survive. It was a terrible time for her. And their mother, Esther Shushan, sat with me. She'd just lost her child, yet she allowed me to photograph her. She looked into my eyes. She shared photographs of Yocheved. She helped me to find the mound of dirt where Yocheved was buried.

I made a commitment to Esther Shushan: Every day I say a blessing for Yocheved.

We can look at hearing the stories of others as healing in a number of different ways. One, we can look at the pain and suffering of others, and it's an easier way to find a way to our own pain. We look at their backyard, and our hearts open, and we find a way to relate that and connect to the people in our lives. Somehow that can sometimes be easier to do than dealing with conflict in our own communities.

Another is art. Art, music, poetry, all of these, are illicit teachers, rather than prescriptive. It allows us to create safe structures. I am allowed to go as far as I'm willing to at any given time. I become my own regulator of the healing of my suffering. I regulate the pace; I enter into a safe environment and decide I can heal for myself. It's a safe way to learn about conflict and how I can be better connected in my own community.

The driving force behind Opening of the Heart is to include the voices of all in a conflict and recognize every party is hurt to some degree. At the heart of every act of violence is an unhealed wound. "Opening of the Heart" means that we all have an opportunity to look at something and feel a sense of compassion. All of us know war, in some form or another—in our homes, in our families, in our communities, or in intractable conflicts around the world. These conflicts offend or traumatize our language skills, our mental structures. Therefore we look to engage people at the place where their deepest fears and joys can be touched, and that place is where the language of the heart is held.

Miriam Shushan, the sister of the Israeli 10-year-old, continues to struggle with operations. Her body is in a lot of ongoing pain, so the trauma is never over for her. We told her about the progress of an Opening of the Heart exhibition we had planned, and let her know that we're moving forward in the world: "We're doing a curriculum with your story." When I revisit people who've been traumatized, at first there's the shock of "You're actually including voices from the other side? Why are you including Arab music? Why are you including Arab voices?" This happens both ways. "Why would you include Israeli voices in your exhibition?" I hear this from people who've been traumatized on the Palestinian side.

The unhealed wound strengthens this conflict. It keeps it in place. It builds on the already existing stereotypes, yet, in the case of my exhibit people, what I notice, what I believe, is that they allowed me to photograph them at times of their deepest tragedy and vulnerability because, in a deeper place, they want to make a contribution to the healing of conflict for all of us.

Crossing No Man's Land

The most challenging situation in the Territories is to actually go from one side to the other. To go from the Palestinian area into an Israeli settlement on foot, it's actually unheard of. You need to create a mini-ceasefire of sorts. It's required that you have the grace of all the parties: the military outpost at the settlement, the Palestinian people on the ground; everyone needs to agree that they will allow you to walk through an area known as No Man's Land. My Palestinian host left me at the barrier where No Man's Land begins, about a mile out from the settlement. I had a long walk to make. As I took one step after another, I knew, I felt that I was taking my life in my hands. I also had an awareness of the soldiers on the one side whom I've come to know and who have welcomed me into their tanks, outposts, and checkpoints, and on the other side, the young Palestinians who carry guns and so forth. They all love the same food, they all have hopes and dreams and they're all looking for the same things: safety for their families, work, and so forth.

It was in this place, where the two sides meet in violence, that the idea for Opening of the Heart was born. I thought, there has to be space for something other than violence in the place where the two sides meet—where two such beautiful peoples are meeting in violence. What else can we create here?

(Editor's Note: Acknowledgments are given to Gene Knudsen Hoffman and Dr. Selena Sermeno Ph.D, whose work in conflict resolution has provided some of the context for the references included in this interview.)

Andrew Himes is the executive producer of the documentary feature film Voices in Wartime, *and director of the short film* Beyond Wartime. *He has written many articles for newspapers, magazines, and web sites, and spent years as a technology book author, editor, and journalist. As manager of the first web team at Microsoft, he helped pioneer that company's embrace of the Internet, and then founded Project Alchemy, a nonprofit that supported social change by using technology to strengthen movement building, communication, and grassroots activism for community-based nonprofit groups.*

Hell-fire and Transcendence

Andrew Himes

From my grandfather, Dr. John R. Rice, I learned about story-telling, poetry, and the importance of expressing love, grief, and joy. He was an old-fashioned, fundamentalist, fire-and-brimstone, country preacher from Texas, and he was the son, himself, of several generations of Baptist preachers. My grandfather's religion was no academic religion, no intellectual exercise in theology or disputation—though he was a theologian who engaged in many polemics about dogma, faith, and belief. His was a religion of the heart and the soul, a religion of the poor and the humble, the brokenhearted and the lost. And he was a preacher because he loved his fellow humans.

As I was growing up, I heard my grandfather preach hundreds of sermons, and each of them was a string of stories—one story or parable or illustration after another. As he preached, he recited poetry, recited long passages of scripture, sang scraps of hymns, and talked to people alive and dead, from his wife sitting in the front pew to his own long-gone mother looking down on him from heaven. In every sermon, he broke into tears a half dozen times as he spoke of his passion for winning lost souls to Jesus.

For my grandfather, his religion, his faith, and the core of his motivation as a pastor, teacher, counselor, and evangelist were all about telling stories and hearing stories and exchanging stories. What I learned from him was that we all make meaning out of the heartache and struggles of our lives, and we do so by constructing a narrative that can contain the sense of what we have seen and experienced. We convey our grief and suffering through storytelling, we communicate our happiness and rejoicing through storytelling, and we teach some of what we have learned from our lives and from each other through storytelling.

But I also learned from my grandfather an absolute, black-and-white morality. He believed that all of us are sinners and doomed to an eternal hell, literally a lake of fire in which we will experience the torments and agony of the damned forever unless we have accepted Jesus into our hearts. For the living, my grandfather had a very strict set of moral categories. Either you were an agent of God and living for the Lord, or you were an agent of the Devil and living for yourself. As humans, we could do evil, or we could do good, but there was little in between. And his own very literal interpretation of the Bible determined the category to which you belonged.

This has a particular relevance to the subject of war and to the human response to war. Violent conflict is perhaps the most extreme and intense collective human activity. As many veterans of combat have said, it is hard to go back to an ordinary life, working in an ordinary job, and living in an ordinary house behind a white picket fence and a patch of green lawn when you've lived at the very edge of human existence in the course of a war, under conditions of duress and danger, terror and exhilaration, and in the company of comrades who have shared that experience with you. Combat provides a peculiar and deadly thrill, even as it rewires the brain and unleashes the nightmares.

As a young man and a civilian during the most tragic and terrible years of the Vietnam War, I understood little or nothing about the experience of the combat veteran. I was deeply opposed to the war and horrified by what I saw on the television evening news and the daily newspaper. I hated the politicians who launched the war and the generals who led the war and the officers and soldiers who participated in the war. And I hated my grandfather who justified the war in the name of God, and who was enraged by those who opposed the war.

He thought of them as hippies, communists, apostates, and agents of the Devil. When I joined the ranks of the peaceniks, I was tarred with their brush. And I proclaimed my own absolute and self-righteous opposition to the pro-war politics of my grandfather.

I would have made any sacrifice during the Vietnam War if I thought it would help to end that war, and I devoted myself completely to the peace movement. I gave up college, forgot about a career and an ordinary life, was arrested several times, and devoted myself to being an activist against the war and then an activist for civil rights and social justice generally in the years that followed the war.

It is interesting to me now to look back on those days and understand that I shared my grandfather's absolute morality and his sense of self righteousness. I believed that U.S. soldiers were engaged in an immoral enterprise—the war in Vietnam—and thus were available for my condemnation. I had little compassion for the suffering of the soldiers themselves, and I failed to understand that they were themselves victims of the war. I refused to look at their motivations, and resisted looking at their sufferings and sorrows, because I thought they had made moral choices that were worthy of my own sanctified disapproval.

I have a history as a fool, and an arrogant one. My foolishness was not to oppose the war, but to oppose the warrior. My arrogance was to imagine that I had a lock on truth, justice, and morality, and that my motives were clean and pure, while those of my opponents were racist, violent, and morally contaminated.

I have learned lessons in the making of the film *Voices in Wartime*. Compassion for the warrior, even as we search for alternatives to the practice of war itself. Regard for the long-term costs borne by the civilian victims of war, and their need for healing, support, and opportunity. Respect and gratitude for the soldier who volunteers to give his life for the health and safety of his community, even as we might decry the policies that thrust him into danger. Love and support for the families of those soldiers, who suffer from their absence and pray for their safe return. Finally, an appreciation for the role of art in general and storytelling in particular in healing the wounds of war and rebuilding the community.

In the end, all we have are the human bonds of love and care that connect us. Those bonds are forged through the telling of our common tale, across the gaps of history, culture and language, through the poems, stories, images, and chaos of our common dilemma—how to listen to each other and work for healing when every instinct tells us to hoard our suspicions and launch preemptive strikes on our enemies.

In the end, the memory of my grandfather that lingers is the one that reveals him most as my kindred soul. In one of his sermons, he told the story of the death of his mother, Sarah LaPrade Rice, when he was a little boy of five:

> "I remember the November day when we lay her body away. My father knelt beside the open grave. There was no white muslin to hide the raw dirt of the grave—like a wound in the earth. No fake, manmade carpet of grass was thrown over the clods. My father put one arm around his two little orphan girls and one around his two little boys, and watched as they lowered the precious body in its dark casket into the bosom of Mother Earth. The rain beat down upon us, and a friendly neighbor held an umbrella over our heads."

In that paragraph, is the core of the grief that remained with him throughout his life, and that fueled his passion to win souls to Jesus. It was an impulse toward redemption, sacrifice, and love, and what he thought of as Heaven itself, in the most literal sense.

In the grief of my grandfather, and in his love and sense of loss, is the seed of compassion that we will all need to heal this damaged world. From Baghdad to Baltimore, from Fallujah to Birmingham, from Jerusalem to Seattle, we connect with each other through what is missing from our lives. We evolve by means of the stories we pass from one to the other, around the circle, close to the fire.

Cameron Penny was in the fourth grade in a Michigan school when he wrote this poem. It was originally published in the November/December 2001 issue of North American Review. *Marie Howe reads his poem in the film* Voices in Wartime.

If You Are Lucky in This Life

If you are lucky in this life
A window will appear on a battlefield between two armies.

And when the soldiers look into the window
They don't see their enemies
They see themselves as children.

And they stop fighting
And go home and go to sleep.
When they wake up, the land is well again.

Cameron Penny

This is a Language Made for Blood

/

Brian Turner

Brian Turner *was an infantry soldier who came off active duty in April 2005. He was an infantry team leader, an NCD, in Iraq for a year beginning November 2003, and served with the 3rd Stryker Brigade Combat Team, 2nd Infantry Division. Prior to that, he deployed to Bosnia-Herzegovina in 1999-2000 with the 10th Mountain Division. Before joing the army, he earned an MFA in Creative Writing (poetry) from the University of Oregon. He has published poetry in several literary reviews, and his book* Here, Bullet *is the winner of the 2005 Beatrice Hawley Award from Alice James Books.*

A Soldier's Arabic

> *This is a strange new kind of war where you learn*
> *just as much as you are able to believe.*
> —E. Hemingway

The word for love, Habib, is written from right
to left, starting where we would end it
and ending where we might begin.

Where we would end a war
another might take as a beginning,
or as an echo of history, recited again.

Speak the word for death, Maut,
and you will hear the cursives of the wind
driven into the veil of the unknown.

This is a language made of blood.
It is made of sand, and time.
To be spoken, it must be earned.

2000 lbs.

Ashur Square, Mosul

It begins simply with a fist, white-knuckled
and tight, glossy with sweat. With two eyes
in a rearview mirror watching for a convoy.
The radio a soundtrack that adrenaline has
pushed into silence, replacing it with a heartbeat,
that of his thumb, shaking over the button.

·

A flight of gold, that's what Sefwan thinks
as he lights a Miami, draws in the smoke
and waits in his taxi at the traffic circle.
Sefwan thinks of the year 1974, the summer
he lifted pitchforks of grain high into the air,
the slow drift of it like the fall of Shatha's hair,
and although it was decades ago, he still loves her,
and there are times like this when he thinks of her
standing at the cane-break where the buffalo cooled
shoulder-deep in the water, and the orange cups
of flowers he brought her, and he wonders
how so much can go wrong in a life, how easy
the years slip by, as light as that grain, as bright
as the street's concussion of metal, the shrapnel
traveling at the speed of sound to open him
in blood and shock, a man whose last thoughts
will be of love and wreckage, a dying man
with no one there to whisper him gone.

·

Sgt. Ledouix of the Washington National Guard
speaks but cannot hear the words coming out,
and it's just as well his eardrums have ruptured
because it lends the world a certain calm,
though the traffic circle is filled with people
running in panic, their legs a colorful blur,
reminiscent of horses in a carousel,
turning and turning the way the tires spin
on the humvee flipped onto its side,
the gunner's hatch he was thrown from
a mystery to him now, a dark hole
in metal the color of sand, and if he could,
he would crawl back inside of it,
though his fingertips scratch at the asphalt
he hasn't the strength to move, and it's true
he's dying, shrapnel has torn into his side
and he will bleed to death in only minutes,
but he finds himself surrounded by a strange
beauty, the shine of light on the broken,
a woman's hand touching his face, tenderly
the way his wife might, amazed to find
their wedding ring on his crushed hand,
the bright gold sinking in flesh
going to bone.

•

Nearby, an old woman cradles her grandson
in her arms, whispering, rocking him there
on her knees, as though singing him to sleep,
her hands wet with their blood, her black dress
soaking in it still as her legs give out
and she buckles with him to the ground,
and if you'd asked her forty years earlier
if she could see herself an old woman
begging by the roadside for money, here,
with a bomb exploding at the market

among all these people, she'd have said
it's impossible, this isn't the way we die
in this life, that there must be something better
than this, to have your heart broken
one last time before dying, to kiss
a child who was given sight of a world
he could never share, and to lay him down
and close her eyes beside him, the shock
chilling her, even with the sun so high
above, she would say it's impossible,
who would do such a thing, who could
design a moment such as this, and believe
war's victories could be worth the loss?

●

When it happens, Rasheed is on his bicycle
passing the bridal shop, with Sefa beside him,
and just before the air ruckles and breaks
he glimpses the sidewalk reflections
in the storefront glass, men and women
walking and talking, pausing in thought, or not,
and all of this takes place in an instant
of clarity, just before each of them shatters
into a thousand pieces under the detonation's wave,
as if the very thought of them were being
completely destroyed, stripping them of form,
that explosive blast tearing into the manikins
who stood as though man and wife a moment before,
who have no eyes or lips, who cannot touch
one another, who cannot even kiss, ever,
who now lie together in glass and debris,
holding one another in their half-armed embrace,
calling this love, if this is all there will ever be.

•

A holy man watches from an acrylic painting
on an adjacent wall, his beard brushed in black,
a headscarf of emerald green, and his eyes,
benevolent and knowing, they take it all in,
the burst of metal, the wounded and the dying,
and what would his answer be if asked
Is this what Mohammed taught, is it this
which earns a country?—because it's difficult
to see in the confusion and dust and rubble,
it's difficult to see the political nuances
in blood, when the blood is before you, or your own,
it's difficult to look away, and has he learned
such power has grief as its price.

•

The civil affairs officer, Lt. Jackson, stares
at his missing hands, which makes
no sense to him, no sense at all, to have
these absurd stumps held up in the air
where just a moment before he'd blown bubbles
out the humvee window, his left hand holding the bottle,
his right hand dipping the plastic ring in soap,
filling the air behind them with floating spheres,
something for the children, something naïve
and young, something beautiful in a city of soldiers,
translucent globes with their iridescent skins
drifting on vehicle exhaust and the breeze
that might lift one day over the Zagros mountains,
that kind of hope, small globes like that,
what may have astonished someone on the sidewalk
just a moment before, to witness one soldier's
brief display of humanity, seven minutes
before Lt. Jackson blacks out from blood loss
and shock, with no one there to bandage
the wounds that would take him all the way home.

•

And the man who pushed the trigger,
who may have invoked the prophet's name,
or not, is obliterated—
he is everywhere, he is of all things here,
his touch is the air taken in, the blast
and the wave, the electricity of shock,
his is the sound the heart makes quick
in the panic's rush, the surge of blood
searching for light and color, that sound
the martyr cries at the tops of the lungs,
the word Inshallah his soul is made of,
his place of death an epicenter of change,
because the man who pushed the trigger
is a flash of light in a world gone suddenly dim.

•

The word habib is left hanging in the air
over Ashur Square, the telephone line
snapped in two, crackling, and it remains
a strange incantation the dead hear
as they wander confused among one another,
learning each other's names, trying to comfort
the living in their grief, trying to console
those who cannot accept this random pain,
whispering the word one to another there
in the rubble and debris, whispering the word
over and over, that it might not be forgotten.

Sadiq

*It is a condition of wisdom in the archer to be patient
because when the arrow leaves the bow, it returns no more.*
—Sa'di

It should break your heart to kill.
It should make you shake and sweat,
nightmare you, strand you out in a desert
of irrevocable desolation, the consequences
seared into the vein, no matter what adrenaline
feeds the muscle its courage, no matter
what god shines down on you, no matter
what crackling pain and anger
you carry in your fists, my friend,
it should break your heart to kill.
It should never be so easy as this.

INDEX

COPYRIGHT & PERMISSION

APPENDIX
The Voices in Wartime Network

~

The Voices in Wartime Network is a permanent, nonprofit organization dedicated to the mission of enabling millions of people to express themselves artistically, to engage with each other to heal the collective trauma caused by war, and to create a less violent world. The Voices in Wartime mission is inspired by the belief that people can and do heal from the suffering of war, and, furthermore, that by creating a willing and active online community, we can help.

The emerging field of trauma studies has uncovered two essential experiences all trauma victims must undertake to recover from their ordeal: creative self-expression and membership in community. Trauma survivors must be allowed to tell the truth about their experiences, and members of the sufferer's community must be encouraged to listen, to remember, and to repeat the story to others. This is what Dr. Jonathan Shay calls the "process of communalizing" trauma; and this is the place where artists and the arts have played a role since the beginning of time.

The artist can play a role in any one of these steps, or in all of them. According to Shay, it isn't even necessary that the artist be the one who personally experienced the trauma. If he or she is able to retell the story in a form that contains enough of the truth, then the person who did experience it can say, "Yes—you were listening. You heard at least some of it. And you retold it with truthfulness and emotion that I can recognize."

But the truth is not always easy to tell or to listen to, even in the best of times. In times of war, it is often less welcome—even in democracies such as ours. Since September 11th, people all over the world find themselves beset by new challenges—political, economic, social, and psychological. As the global war on terror expands, the resources to deal with the inevitable fallout shrink. Already understaffed and under funded VA hospitals and Vet centers are overwhelmed by soldiers returning from Iraq and Afghanistan suffering from severe emotional trauma and physical injuries.

Help for the families of returning soldiers is even scarcer. Meanwhile, there is a huge, almost invisible population of refugees from all over the world—Vietnam, Somalia, Sudan, Guatemala, Colombia, Iraq, Afghanistan, to name just a few—whose trauma goes unrecognized and untreated, often to the detriment of their own communities and the larger society that surrounds them.

The Voices in Wartime Network web site, voicesinwartime.org, provides an Internet-based platform for all people who have suffered as a result of war to create and share their artwork and connect with one another to share strategies for dealing with the aftermath of violent conflict.

— Andrew Himes

ABOUT WHIT PRESS

Whit Press is a Seattle-based, nonprofit publishing organization dedicated to the transformational power of the written word.

We create books that use literature as a tool in support of other nonprofit organizations working toward environmental and social justice.

Whit Press also exists as an oasis to nurture and promote the rich diversity of literary work from women writers, writers from ethnic and social minorities, young writers, and first-time authors.

We are dedicated to producing beautiful books that combine outstanding literary content with design excellence.

Whit Press brings you the best of fiction, creative nonfiction, and poetry from diverse literary voices who do not have easy access to quality publication.

We publish stories of creative discovery, cultural insight, human experience, spiritual exploration, and more.

 For more information visit our web site:
www.whitpress.org

Whit Press gratefully acknowledges the generous support of our individual contributors and the following organizations:
- **The Breneman-Jaech Foundation**
- **The Seattle Foundation**
- **Seattle Office of Arts & Cultural Affairs**